I0134800

I See You

**Exploring How Our Perceptions
Affect Our Actions**

Michael Carter

Absolute Author
Publishing House

I SEE YOU
Copyright © 2020 by **Michael Carter**
ALL RIGHTS RESERVED

All rights reserved. No part of this publication may be reproduced, distributed, or transmitted in any form or by any means without prior written permission by the author.

Unless otherwise specified, all Scripture quotations are taken from the New King James Version ®. Copyright © 1982 by Thompson Nelson, Inc. Used by permission. All rights reserved.

Publisher: Absolute Author Publishing House
Editor: Dr. Melissa Caudle
Associate Editor: Kathy Rabb Kittok

LIBRARY OF CONGRESS CATALOGUE IN-PUBLICATION-DATA

I SEE YOU/Michael Carter

   p.cm.

Paperback ISBN: 978-1-64953-108-7
eBook ISBN: 978-1-64953-109-4

   1.   Self-help   2. Spiritual   3. Religion   4. Humanity

PRINTED IN THE UNTIED STATES OF AMERICA

A great collection of reflections from a pastor that I greatly admire and respect. Though an easy read, it requires deep reflection over the themes so well captured by the author. Allow the readings to sharpen your perceptions of current issues such as color, race, privilege, religion, and politics. I see myself, is a must-read section for all teenagers. Adults alike should read the book – it will challenge and possibly change your view of the world!

Dr. James Kigamwa, Bridge to Reading, Director

DEDICATION

I dedicate this book to the next generation. With all the wisdom of an older generation has to pass on to the next, there is an equal amount of learning to be absorbed from the younger generation. If an older generation is the foundation of a society, young people are the heartbeat of that society. Although people often joke about the fact that a young person's frontal cortex isn't fully developed until about age twenty-five, which may help explain the roller coaster journey of a teenager, it should also be noted that many people had accomplished great things before their brain was developed:

- Nyeeam Hudson has traveled the world, delivering motivational speeches to other kids, offering support to victims of bullying, building up confidence, and teaching self-love.
- Marley Dias started *#1000BlackGirlBook* campaign at age 13
- Louis Braille invented the Braille System at Age 15
- Laura Dekker sailed around the world solo at Age 14
- Nadia Comaneci received a perfect ten at Age 14 at the Olympics
- Malala Yousafzai won the Nobel Peace Prize at Age 17
- Pelé won the World Cup at Age 17

- Jacob Barnett gave one of the most popular TED Talks at Age 14
- Suhas Gopinath became the world's youngest CEO at Age 17
- Mark Zuckerberg founded Facebook at Age 19
- Annie Oakley was a champion sharpshooter at Age 15
- Katherine Johnson (famous for her work at NASA) graduated high school at age 14 and earned a double degree in math and French from West Virginia State College at age 18

To name a few. I salute you, young people, and encourage you to use your youthful fearlessness to do something great.

Acknowledgments

The world becomes a better place when individuals seek to serve others as they pursue their interests in their journey. On my journey, I had the tremendous privilege of having open and meaningful conversations with a group of young world-changers. The following people have collectively been an invaluable resource in searching for a call to action for global social change, with their ideas, self-reflection, and transparency. This book, years in the making, would not have come to fruition without them. The words "Thank you" seem immensely insufficient to convey my sentiment toward them. But those words are all I have. In no particular order, I would like to thank the following individuals for their contribution to this work.

Alex Baker
Alondra Quezada
Amanda Middleton
Angel Rodriguez
Angela DiCristo
Angelica Weaver
Annastasia Shufford
Ariana Milla Ramirez
Braxton Reichard
Caitlyn Klinepeter-Persing
Christina Colón
Chris Ortiz
Ciara Goodbar

DaQueisha Epps
Darnisha Graves
Destiny Babilonia
Donnesha Robinson
Jesse Hernandez
Jessica Rodriguez
Kerri Hojem
Kolten Turner
Lexi Palmer
Lilly Garard
Linnea Chilman
Makenzie Healy
Manasse Kwete

Marie Hugershoff
Michael D. Carter
Mohammed Khaled-
Mohammed
Morgan Hale
Nia Carter
Nicole Gonzalez
Nifemi Adejumobi
Qiandong Xu (Amos)

Renee Carter
Roxana Mendoza
Samantha Karichu
Seniqua Carter
Shala Carter
Tony Gruenloh
Yulia Nefedova
Zach Goodbar
Zina Teague

TABLE OF CONTENTS

INTRODUCTION

You can't see who you don't know, and you can't know who you don't see.

The level of our relationship with people, how we relate to people, how we elevate and are elevated by people, how we treat people, close to us or not, our choice of words when we talk to people, and our attitude toward people, all stem from our perception of people.

Understanding is one of the many keys to peaceful coexistence, and it is also one key to every successful relationship. For you to relate well with other humans, you need to have some level of understanding of the person or people you want to relate to. You need to exercise patience while attempting to gain an appreciation for them. When you cannot be patient while gaining an understanding of others, you become easily annoyed with their words and actions, especially those words and actions that contradict your own.

MICHAEL CARTER

UNDERSTANDING

I realize that the most challenging thing for humans is to relate to other humans! We can seek and subsequently gain some level of understanding when it comes to the cosmos, science, the human body, agriculture, and so many other mysteries. But what happens to that ability when it comes to dealing with other humans? What happened to take the time to understand each other or taking time to understand our perception of people, and why we have those perceptions?

My world differs from your world; your friend's world differs from your world; my friend's world differs from my world, and so forth. Our worldviews differ from each other. Why, then, do we have issues with each other based on inherent differences? Why do we mistreat each other? Why do we hate each other? The answer to these questions, in part, is a lack of understanding. We don't take the time to understand each other. Some people may not feel that we must gain a greater understanding of each other, but as long as people keep each other at arms distance when it comes to who we are and why we feel and think the way we do, we will always have problems that divide us.

Like so many others, I judged people based on their race, political views, and even gender while growing up. I realize that you cannot judge people by comparing your lifestyle with theirs. We remember that everyone is created differently, with diverse gifts and talents, characteristics, aspirations, and purposes. Over time, we all develop a worldview that may differ from everyone else's worldview.

In 2019, twenty people were killed, and many others were injured in a Walmart in El Paso, Texas. The massacre, seemingly domestic terrorism, was called one of the deadliest mass shootings in US history. It was discovered that the shooter posted a manifesto claiming a "Hispanic Invasion of Texas," and he "wanted to shoot as many Mexicans as possible."

To many people, an act like this is appalling and unthinkable. Most of us would struggle to make sense of it. According to psychologist Arash Emamzadeh, one psychological theory suggests when we perceive that our group is in direct competition with another, especially over a limited resource, we are likely to experience hostility toward members of that group. This is the "Us vs. Them" mentality. One problem with this mentality is that it distorts complicated issues by separating the world into them and us, and them makes "them" the scapegoat and, consequently, the villain.

When it comes to humanity, mostly, this perception is wrong and has caused strife and division between people. Ernest Hemingway said, "When people speak, listen completely to them." Most people do not have the patience to listen; they only want to hear the first sentence you speak so they can judge you based on a soundbite. One necessary, but infinitely valuable lesson that I have learned is that it is always better to be quick to hear and slow to respond. As my mother used to say, "That's why God gave you two ears and one mouth!"

Having a "quick to hear and slow to speak" mentality allows you to take time to process what you heard and your thoughts before responding.

F. Scott Fitzgerald, speaking of advice that his father gave him, said, "Whenever you feel like criticizing anyone," he told me, "just remember that all the people in this world haven't had the advantages you've had." Why criticize people because of who they are? Why attack people because of what they are? Why blame people because they are not up to your standard? In my estimation, there is only one divine standard, and none of us are living up to it.

You fail to take the time and attempt to understand those that are not like you cause you to relate to people based on your perceptions of them. It leads you to treat people based on their color or their background and to neglect people because of their status in society. A lack of understanding, especially related to the "us vs. them" mentality, is not new; we know that. However, I genuinely believe that through self-reflection, humility, and selfless sacrifice, you and I can find a solution, or at least lay a foundation that the next generation can continue to build on. It will require each of us to reevaluate our worldview; to examine how you came to believe what you believe about society and others, especially those who are not like you. Does your identity lay in your societal group membership, or something else?

I SEE YOU

Lutheran pastor and theologian Dietrich Bonhoeffer once said, "We must know how to respect people less because of what they do or omit to do, and more because of what they suffer." In this book, you learn that to affect change, you must first seek to understand yourself and that the world only becomes a better place when you and I strive to understand others.

"I See You" is a book that will cause you to pause and analyze your perceptions of others. This book explores and hopefully reveals the perceptions you have about others and yourself. It explores how you treat people that think and act differently than you and how you approach relationships. I hope that this book will inspire you to separate your perceptions of others from your treatment of others, paving the way for unity and peaceful coexistence in society.

"I See You" goes beyond these three words.

CHAPTER 1:
I SEE COLOR

Color is a power which directly influences the soul. - **Wassily Kandinsky**

I remember being seventeen and trying to decide if I wanted to take on student loan debt and go to college, or just get a job, or do something else with my life. I decided against my mothers' unspoken but visible disapproval to join the U.S. Army; hey, they did more before 9:00 a.m. than most people did all day, and for some strange reason, that excited me.

It was the fall of 1984, and I was both excited and frightened as I went down to the Military Entrance Processing Station **(M.E.P.S.)** Center to go through my entrance examinations. That day I walked like a duck, answered questions about my "remains" in the unlikely event I was killed in battle, discussed my job preferences,

1

and took several mental and physical tests. I happened upon one testing station in particular, where a polite young woman began asking me questions about what I saw on a series of cards she had placed in front of me. As I stared blankly at the cards, I thought, *Is this some mind game?* Maybe it is the psychological exam that everyone has to endure to see if you're mentally fit for service. Or perhaps it's a test to see if you'll crack under pressure if captured by the enemy.

On the cards were a bunch of beautiful, colorful dots of all sizes. When the Specialist asked me, "What do you see?" I wanted to say, "I see a myriad of colorful confusion," however, I knew that, most likely, this wasn't the answer she was looking for. Judging by the blank look on her face, it was safe to assume that she didn't have much sense of humor. And since I didn't want to take the chance of ending up in the brig before I even got to basic training, I answered, "Dots."

It quickly became apparent that this wasn't the answer she was looking for either. Her blank stare faded into what appeared to be a menacing scowl, and in a very low, monotone, and somewhat threatening voice, she said, "Are you serious?"

"I think so," I said. "What do you see in the dots?"

It became painfully apparent that I was colorblind, or more accurately, color vision deficient. Once my friends found this out, they felt a dutiful obligation to test me for themselves to see if this outlandish claim could be valid.

I SEE YOU

What color is that wall? What color is my shirt? What color is that car over there? Then came the pity; they felt so sorry for me. How could I go on living without being able to distinguish color properly? How could I get dressed, or how would I know if I'm eating green vegetables or not? How could I tell the difference between mustard and cheese? Thankfully, it was discovered that my condition was a red-green deficiency or mild deuteranomaly, and I could live an everyday healthy life. However, I might have trouble diffusing a bomb, and would always wonder if I was eating an orange when I thought it was a peach.

Most people who are considered "color blind" can see colors. Still, specific colors may appear washed out and are easily confused with other colors, depending on the color vision deficiency they have. I have, however, learned that seeing color is not only beneficial to living a functional life, but it is enjoyable. It is also something that I believe we take for granted (ask a color vision deficient person). Unless you're a fashion designer, artist, interior decorator, or perhaps a person trying to determine whether to cut the red or green wire, the thought of purposefully focusing on color doesn't dominate your thought life daily. The renowned paint manufacturer Valspar produced a video a few years ago promoting glasses that EnChroma developed. These glasses would help people who deal with color blindness see color. The very emotional video highlights just how awe-inspiring color is, and what an excellent experience color can be. Most people who see color probably take it for granted.

MICHAEL CARTER

We often see color everywhere except in ourselves.

In humans, I appreciate people who make the heartfelt statement that they **don't see color** in those of another race. The implication is that the person doesn't discriminate or is not prejudiced against someone else because of their race or skin color. While this genuine sentiment strikes a chord with the human heart and cultivates unity among races, I find a fundamental and ultimately dividing flaw in its intent. Just as we appreciate awesome sunsets, beautiful flowerbeds, exquisite art, and imaginative clothing, we must also enjoy all the colors God created in humans.

In 2001, I was privileged to go on a mission trip with several other men to Haiti. There were six White men and five Black men, the right mix. When we landed in Port Au Prince, one of the first things that we noticed was all the locals hanging around at the airport. Once we collected our luggage, we began walking to the parking lot to meet the van that would carry us to our destination. To get to the parking lot, we had to follow a path confined by ropes, much like being at Disney World waiting to get on a ride. As we were making our way through the line to the waiting van, I gazed out at all the people who were mostly brown-skinned Haitians, and (that reason undoubtedly being the color of their skin), I felt a connection. With all the racial tension in America, I almost felt more comfortable because I'm now in a place where most people looked like me. We had the same skin color so that we would hit it off, couldn't we? Just then, something interesting happened. One of the Haitian guards waved one of my Black friends over to him, showing that he could jump over the rope, so he wouldn't have to endure the long line. As my friend made his way over the rope, that same guard spotted me and waved me over. Right behind me was another man in our group who was White. He noticed that we were receiving a favor, and not wanting to stand in the line enduring the near one-hundred-degree heat, he followed me over, assuming that we would all be able to jump the rope. It never occurred to me that he was waving my friend and me over because we had the same skin color that he had.

As I jumped the rope, the guard promptly stopped my White friend, saying, "No, you cannot come!" I asked, "Why?" and the guard only replied, "blan, blan!"

I surmised that this must be the Creole word for White. My friend, who was ahead of me, was already over the rope, but instead of climbing over, I declined, saying I would wait with my other friends in line. Just then, something occurred to me; an epiphany, a "wow" moment, a revelation. As I looked around at the cornucopia of people, most of whom had brown skin, I realized that other than skin color, I didn't relate to these people at all. I understood that I had more in common with the men I came with, Black and White, than all of my brothers here in Haiti. I didn't have any bad feelings toward the people there, not at all. It just occurred to me I may search for something using the wrong metrics. Instead of using color alone to form a connection with another human being, I realized that we should quantify our meaningful

5

relationships with things like beliefs, core values, shared interests, and relatability. Sure, there are intangible and intrinsic characteristics stemming from the race that draw people together, which can't be denied. Similarly, there are some noticeable cultural differences, like food, slang, family structure, music, clothing, etc. But when those factors far outweigh core values, it can cause an unnecessary divide that will gain momentum with time.

Judging vs. Racism

One mistake I made, especially as a young person, was to assume that judging someone who had different color skin than mine was the same as racism. While judging someone based on the color of their skin can lead to discrimination, it is not the same. Let's look at two standard terms and one not so common.

Race can be defined as "a family, tribe, people, or nation belonging to the same stock."
Racism can be defined as the belief that "racial differences produce an inherent superiority of a particular race."

Colorism, a term believed to be first coined in 1982 by Pulitzer Prize winner Alice Walker, which means "the prejudicial or preferential treatment of same-race people based solely on their color."[4]

I have witnessed discriminatory social treatment by people of different skin color within the same race. No matter what race you are, you may have observed certain "cliques" in high school or social circles in college or the workplace. Treating other people differently based on the color of their skin may not be restricted to those of a distinct race. They have to have a different skin color.

Passing judgment on another individual by the color of their skin alone is not the result of wading in shallow racial waters. By that, I mean that you wouldn't observe someone who has a different skin color and, with no outside influence, automatically conclude about that person based on what you see. It comes from many factors, including upbringing, environment, media, history, and fear, to name a few. It is an issue that has probably existed since the first humans who had different skin colors came to that very realization. Still, I don't believe it is an issue that we should accept as the status quo. Just because something has always been, doesn't mean it always has to be. To animate a change in forming opinions about others based solely on the color of their skin, we must take a hard look at why it happens. It would be a daunting task to examine the history of the world related to racial prejudice and its origin. However, what we can do is start with ourselves (no matter what color you are). I'm sure that many people would like to believe that they don't judge others based on color, but a closer examination of ourselves may reveal that we do just that. Where do our own "color assessments" or rather assumptions come from?

In his book, "Strength to Love," Martin Luther King Jr. makes the following assessment as it relates to racial discrimination in the 1960s, "There are soft-minded persons who would argue that racial segregation should be perpetuated. Negros lag in academic, health, and moral standards. They are not tough-minded enough to realize that lagging measures result from segregation and discrimination. He says, "They do not recognize that it is rationally unsound and sociologically untenable to use the traffic effect of segregation as an argument for its continuation."[5]

Often, we, as rational people, have logical reasons for our assessments of others. We use inductive reasoning to support our judgments and then "drop the mic." Although our conclusions may be based on valid arguments, judging people by their skin color can be like saying, "My mom never listens to me, my friends' mom never listens to her, my neighbors' mom never listens to him. Therefore, all moms fail at listening to their children."

We know that this can't be true. Being a mom doesn't inherently cause you to be a poor listener when it comes to your children. Therefore, inductive reasoning should not be used to judge people of a particular color. I base it on specific instances and often produce weak and invalid arguments. Likewise, color alone shouldn't be used to judge a person. As it relates to people, color alone is not something that should judge; rather, it should be valued. Color is both profound and complicated. The well-known French Impressionist Claude Monet once said, "Color is my day-long obsession, joy, and torment." [6] If we are not careful, we can fall into one of the two categories: we can conclude people because of the color of their skin, not valuing the whole person, or we will discount their color altogether in an attempt not to appear prejudice. This second category doesn't seem as harmful. However, this ultimately brings about an unwitting effort to conform to the other person to ourselves. This can sometimes lead to a more significant division than not valuing the whole person.

American contemporary menswear designer John Varvatos said, "A black suit can be classic and timeless and for most occasions. But remember, it's not so much the color of a suit as it is about the fit, cut, style, and attitude you have when wearing it."

When we look at another person, we see color even if we're one of the many color deficient people. Maybe instead of saying, "I don't see color," the correct phrase would be, "I don't *judge* based on color alone." And while color is a big part of a person's makeup, which helps define who they are, it is not the only thing that defines them. A person can be explained by various attributes, including environment, upbringing, race, beliefs, friends, color, vocabulary, dreams, and so many more things. Therefore, when it comes to the color of a person's skin, we must see it and appreciate it without using it as a unique tool to judge another person.

CHAPTER 2

I SEE JUDGEMENT

"Our judgments judge us, and nothing reveals us, [or] exposes our weaknesses, more ingenious than the attitude of pronouncing upon our fellows." **- Paul Valery**

We've explored how judging someone based on their color alone is probably not the best way to assess them. A big question for me has always been, "Is it ok to judge others?"

Like many others, while growing up, I was encouraged *not* to judge other people. However, you and I know that many people make judgments about others all the time. I'm not sure that it is possible to encounter people without forming some judgment. It would be like asking you to look at these words in parentheses without reading them; just look at them for five seconds: (DO NOT READ ME). It's almost impossible not to read them, no matter how hard you try or how sincere you are in your efforts. I imagine it isn't easy to judge people when we encounter them. Thankfully, many judgments are non-threatening; however, others can be hazardous. When we make judgments without gathering facts, without asking pertinent questions, and without allowing for some amount of time to get to know someone, our decisions can become precariously unbalanced. While it may be necessary for us to judge people, we cannot allow ourselves to make incorrect or uninformed judgments.

The dictionary defines the word judgment as "*The process of forming an opinion or evaluation by discerning and comparing.*" [8] Based on the dictionary definition, judging is a process. It is, in part, a sequence of steps that eventually leads to a particular end, achieved by discerning and comparing. Many people would probably agree that, when it comes to judging people, often, most of us skip to the "particular end" while eschewing the process of discernment. People often assess others based on many factors, such as looks, gender, dress, race, culture, vocabulary, career, and many other characteristics.

While observing others is necessary, premature assessment can eventually lead to avoidable conflict. When you watch, you're "noting," but what many people may not realize is that you determine something or someone's importance or value when you assess.

Imagine your peers are honoring you. They get together, buy a greeting card, and they all sign it and then present it to you. I'm sure, like most people, you would appreciate the gesture. You might take the greeting card home, set it on the kitchen table, or put it on your desk at work. But then, after some time goes by, you would throw it away. Although it was a gracious gesture, it is a greeting card, and they don't last forever. Now imagine your peers all pitched in and got an oversized greeting card on embossed paper. Each of them wrote something unique about you on the card, and then they had the giant card encased in a glass case before presenting it to you during a ceremony. Now, what would you do with the card? You might take it home and put it on the fireplace mantle or place it somewhere where everyone could see it. You probably wouldn't think of throwing it away after a few days or weeks. It would be a keepsake.

Why? Because of the value, you appointed it. When we judge people, we most often assess them and unknowingly assign value to them, and how we treat them can be traced directly to how we value them.

How Judging Relates to the Treatment of Others

How we treat others is essential to our well-being as the food we eat, the career we choose, and the environment we find ourselves. Lolly Daskal, President and CEO of Lead from Within, says, "How you treat others is how you invite them to treat you." In the same article, she says, "If you want to know how others treat you, the best starting place is to look at how you treat others. And if you don't like the way you're treated, there's only one course of action—to change your behavior, because you can't change anyone else's. Relationships function like a mirror—eventually, that change will reflect on how you are treated." [9]

Many of us are familiar with the cliché "You reap what you sow." A passage in the Bible put it this way, "…whatever you plant is what you'll harvest. (Galatians 6:7 GW)" How would you treat people differently if you realized that how you are treated could be a direct result from how you treat others? That this principle wasn't just a virtuous concept, karma, or the universes' way of balancing itself. Maybe some people don't care about how they are treated, but for those of us who do, the "why" is perhaps a little more complex than we realize.

Consider the words of Jesus in this passage from the Bible, "Never criticize or condemn it will all come back on you. Go easy on others; then, they will do the same for you. For if you give, you will get it! Your gift will return to you in a full and overflowing measure, pressed down, shaken together to make room for more, and running over." (Luke 6:37-38 TLB)." It is more than evident that learning to abnegate judgment of people based on our initial assumptions about them is not easy. We judge each other every day.

I had the privilege of having many conversations with an eclectic mix of beautiful people willing to be transparent about many personal subjects, including judgment. One of the many things I realized is that the cause and effect of

MICHAEL CARTER

"people judgment" are often both common and flawed.
Take a moment and examine the following list compiled
from those conversations, and determine if you've ever
been judged in this way, you've considered others in this
way, or perhaps both:

- My family has money, <u>so</u> I'm entitled and snobby.

- I'm loud, <u>so</u> I'm dumb and not well educated.

- I'm loud, <u>so</u> I'm aggressive and scary.

- I'm Mexican, <u>so</u> I eat tacos.

- I'm a black woman, <u>so</u> I'm angry.

- I'm white, <u>so</u> I'm privileged.

- I dress nicely, <u>so</u> I'm stuck up.

- I'm not religious, <u>so</u> I don't have morals.

- I don't emphasize my clothes, <u>so</u> I don't care about
life.

- I'm a black man, <u>so</u> I'm not a hard worker.

- I'm homeless, <u>so</u> I'm lazy.

- I'm a Christian, <u>so</u> I'm sheltered, boring, and
judgmental.

- I get A's & B's in school, <u>so</u> I'm a nerd.

- I'm overweight, <u>so</u> I'm apathetic.

- I'm white, <u>so</u> I'm racist.

- I'm religious, <u>so</u> I'm close-minded.

- I'm an introvert, <u>so</u> I'm weird.

- I'm an extrovert, <u>so</u> I lack restraint.

- I'm a jock, <u>so</u> I'm shallow and reckless.

Do any of these statements, or variations of these statements, resemble the way you've felt you were being judged? Or maybe even compare thoughts that have crossed your mind about others? If so, you're not alone. Most everyone person I interviewed related to one or more of these statements! According to **Elizabeth R. Thornton**, author of *The Objective Leader: How to Leverage the Power of Seeing Things as They Are,* and Founder of the Global Initiative for Objective Leadership, Inc. says that most people are misjudged or misjudge others all the time.[12] She says in an online article that:

> "The reality is many of us misjudge people—often—sometimes based on what they look like, what they are wearing, or perhaps what they sound like. My objectivity survey revealed that 75 percent

15

of the class or workshop participants responded that they misjudged someone at least once a month or more. The survey also found that 23.4 percent said they misjudged someone based on their appearance two or three times per month; 9.4 percent said once a month; 17.4 percent said two or three times per week, and 4.7 percent said they misjudged someone based on their appearance every day."

That's more misjudgment. If I were honest with myself, I would say that I am probably not different from many workshop participants. Those of us who fall into one or more of those categories may not even realize that we're misjudging people so often. While "nobody's perfect," we're going to underestimate people from time to time, realizing that it can have a lasting negative effect on others may help us pay more attention to how often we judge.

Judgment is Not Upsetting Until Someone Judges You

I remember growing up in Columbus, Ohio, and how being an Ohio State Buckeyes fan was more like a religion than it was community entertainment. I was and still am an avid Buckeye fan. So, when the opportunity to sell refreshments and the OSU football games for an entire season presented itself, a friend and I jumped at the chance. After we worked a few games, he came up with a bright idea. He mentioned that during each game, things became so hectic that if we were to sell our first rack of Coca-Cola, and then put down the shelves and walk out, no one would ever notice. In just a few minutes, we could have an apron full of money (a whole $30), which would be more than we could make in two games. I explained that I thought this was a terrible idea because I didn't care how much money I made. I was still in shock that I got in the stadium for free, and mostly, I could watch a good portion of each game. I was in heaven! I loved football and loved the Buckeyes even more. I was the guy that the fans would yell at saying, "Hey, how about a coke over here," and I'd yell back, "sure, hang on, after this play!"

That didn't go over too well, but I did just enough to keep my job. The job was great, and I love people, so I talked and joked with everyone I encountered, whether they were buying refreshments or not. In the office, I was the life of the party because I was so happy to be in "The Horseshoe" (Ohio State's football stadium). One Saturday, my friend finally convinced me to join in his caper. I still knew it was a bad idea, but he was a natural leader, and I was a genuine follower. So, we sold our first rack of Coca Cola, put down our shelves, and went into the bathroom to pocket the money. Just as we walked out, a pleasant gentleman entered the bathroom and asked, "Going somewhere?" He worked for the university, and with that, we were busted! I'm telling this story because of what happened next. He didn't call the police, he didn't get our parents, nor did he take us back to the office. He confiscated our aprons and the money and escorted us to the exit, where we were banished from the Horseshoe forever. I was devastated! To add to my pain, an interesting thing happened on our way to the exit.

The man put his arm around my friend, and in earshot of me said, "I see what's going on here. Your friend is very charismatic and convinced you to do this. Let me give you some advice, stay away from people like him."

What? Are you kidding me? *He* was the one that convinced *me*! My friend stayed silent and just shook his head. After we left the stadium, he laughed all the way home. I was fuming! It was not because we got busted, nor because my friend was laughing (we were childhood friends, so I expected as much), but because that guy thought I was outgoing, I must be the one behind the escapade. Because I'm an extrovert, *I* would be the one behind it if there were any mischief. I was more upset that I'd been *judged* unfairly than I was at getting caught.

Judging others unfairly can have a similar impact on discrimination. Those who are unfairly judged may feel isolated, ashamed, misunderstood, criticized, or demeaned. It can also lead to people being less likely to discuss what they're going through, which hinders them from getting help. And while fair judgment can be a useful tool in enhancing our own life, an unfair decision not only affects the one being judged but can negatively affect the judging. In his article, *Why Judging Others Is Bad for You,* Dr. Rubin Khoddam says that "We, as humans, fuse with our judgments and perceive them as reality."

He says, "We fuse, meaning that we can't tell the difference between what our opinion is and what the reality is. And our perception becomes our reality."

However, this is not a universal reality. "We end up believing our thoughts or judgments and take our thoughts as facts." As I think about this, I realize that our judgments are too often conveyed destructively rather than stating how we feel. For example, you may look at a married person and say, "Wow, that person is ugly; how did they get someone to marry them?" Well, someone found them at least attractive enough to marry. Maybe it's not "that person is ugly," instead "*I* don't find that person attractive."

I understand that this can very well be viewed as semantics. Both statements express the same sentiment. However, one of them leaves room for other people's opinions.

There is an old English-language children's' rhyme that you may have heard before; it goes like this. "Sticks and stones may break my bones, but words will never hurt me." Remember that old saying? It is a familiar childhood chant that means hurtful words cannot cause physical pain, so that I will ignore them. You can't hurt me by calling me names. This can be a very helpful adage to deal with judgments that people may have about you. In our life, all of us will deal with names, words, and decisions about us that are incorrect and meant to be hurtful. It is beneficial to remember that they are someone else's opinion and that we, not other people, play the most significant role in our life success. However, we cannot ignore the fact that what people think about us affects us. Likewise, what you say about others, and how you judge other people affects them somehow, whether negative or positive.

CHAPTER 3

I SEE MYSELF

"The minute you learn to love yourself, you won't want to be anyone else." – **Rihanna**

Michael Jackson was an enigma. The dancer and singer had a significant number of hits that outlived him. One of his most famous hit songs was "Man in The Mirror." As children and young adults, we sang and danced to this song. However, besides having a great vibe, the music contained one of the most important messages out there -- What is within affects what is without! This concept seems simple enough. It is so simple that it is often overlooked or taken for granted. The mind is so powerful that we can hardly fathom what it is fully capable of doing.

As humans, one vital lesson we need to learn is that we are in control of who and what we allow to hurt us. As Eleanor

I SEE YOU

Roosevelt so eloquently put it, "No one can hurt you without permission from yourself." The question is, "Why is the mind so powerful?"

Well, look at it this way; the mind affects how we see ourselves. Therefore, unintelligent people can believe they are smart. It is also why an obedient child raised in a household where they are frequently called "naughty" would assume that they are naughty. This belief, which is now ingrained into them, affects how they see themselves and see others. That little seed, the self-image you have of yourself, involves much more than what is inside you.

Everyone has a perception of life. We all see life in our own unique and individual ways. That perception results from all the things you have gone through to make you who you are. Those experiences, advice taken and rejected, and a plethora of other things, help to form the person you are.

I knew a woman who was a pet lover, and she told me about a time when she moved into a small flat to save money and work. She decided to get a pet, a cat. Getting a cat was a big deal for her. Before that decision, she had been an avid dog lover. In her past, she had little to do with cats because she perceived cats as standoffish and snobbish animals that only came around when they felt like it. As someone who had enjoyed undying love and affection from dogs, the thought of an animal that didn't adore her and show its constant, undying affection didn't interest her. However, she was lonely in her new apartment, and the apartment wasn't suitable for a dog, so she chose a cat. She had low expectations where affection was concerned. However, she was wrong. She got her kitten when he was eight weeks old, so it was small. Yet, his previous owners had bathed him with so much love that he settled right in. They had loved him and petted him so much that he saw himself as part of a family. He saw himself as a loved pet. He didn't understand the concept of danger or fear because of his experiences. Life had been one picnic right from the start, and so even when he was thrust into the unfamiliar arms of a stranger, he settled right in.

A few months down the line, she was offered another kitten that was barely a month old. It was so small that it fits into her palm. He had been abandoned and forced to live with other kittens. They were fed little food and water. They had taught the kitten early that he was replaceable, and he received a meagre share of food and water. The first time she placed a meal in front of him, he growled loudly and terribly for such a tiny creature and grabbed the bowl as if it were his last meal. He refused to cuddle even when he saw her cuddling with the other kitten. He treated the other kitten as a rival and would battle for things he felt were rightly his, which the other kitten didn't even want. He viewed life as war, as a battle, and so continuously, he fought, even when there was no need to act this way.

Like those two kittens, we all have varying perspectives of ourselves, others, and life. Those perspectives form the basis of how we act. They also form the basis of what we passionately believe. These perceptions affect how we see others and, ultimately, how we work toward them. If you see yourself as ordinary, replaceable, and nothing special, you will see everyone else as competition, and you would treat them as a person treats a game. It would appear that solves this perception issue. We have to change the way we see ourselves, and all would be well. However, it isn't that simple. This is because, throughout our lives, we are exposed to various positive and negative experiences. We often cannot push past the negativity to create the image of ourselves that we want- the picture that we need.

Myself and Rejection

Rejection! Unless you were that rich and good-looking kid who was brainy too, you have experienced rejection on some level. Even if you were that rich, brainy, and handsome kid, you could still have gotten rejected because not everyone has excellent taste. Eliminating rejection is impossible. Some sacrifices teach us growth. Some are the saving graces that do not allow us to embark on paths that would hurt us in the long run. However, some are plain and simple rejections that hurt terribly.
The key is to see rejection as part of growth. Realize that sacrifices are necessary for growth. When a company embarks on a project to reach a particular aim or create a specific item, rarely do they go with their first idea. What they come up with is often passed through a panel, analyzed, and critiqued. It does not do this because the original image is senseless; instead, it is done because it knows that there can be more and that it can be better.

When you face rejection, realize that it is not a reflection of who you are. The fact that you do not fit into the specification of someone's or something's needs or desires does not mean that you are a failure. You will not be right for everyone or everything, and this is a fact. This is not because of your inadequacies. Instead, it is because of the unique set of characteristics that makes you who you are is tailored to meet specific requirements and suit particular tastes. You are not built for everything. The moment you fit into every place is the moment you lose the actual place you belong to. A master key is a great example. While it can be used in every situation, realize that there is always a key designed with that door in mind. The master key is only necessary when the first one is not available.

Sometimes, let go of an idea or opportunity that you were looking forward to seeing to fruition.

"But, I want it…"

Unfortunately, you cannot help that. Rejection is painful. It takes a unique ability to look through the pain and see the silver lining. When a denial occurs, the big question is, **_Do I improve, or do I overlook it_**?" To answer these questions, you must learn to place rejection into two categories: constructive and destructive.

Constructive and Destructive Rejection

Constructive rejection helps you improve. They could come from well or ill-meaning sources. The key is to filter out emotion and look at the reason you were rejected.

Were you left because the position required a better you or because the situation didn't require you at all? Look into your long-term goals. Does the thing you were aiming to fit into the long-term image you have of yourself? Constructive rejection builds you up. It is the type that encourages you to improve and try again. **However, violent rejection** usually comes from a place of impure intentions. This rejection has less to do with whom you are and more to do with whom the rejecting person is. You will not be good enough for some people, which is fine because you do not need them. Pick whatever lessons you can from the ordeal and move on. Do not allow anyone's requirement to make you feel like a failure. Somewhere, there is someone who is seeking the best version of you. You need to:

1. Reach for and realize the best version of you.
2. Look for the right fit that deserves you.

Lastly, remember, do not allow the rejection of others, constructive or not, cause you to reject yourself. The first step to improvement is acceptance. Accept the positives and accept that you need to change the negatives. This is how you improve.

Myself and Hatred

What happens when you allow the circumstances and the rejection of external factors to cause you to reject yourself or weigh you down? Simple; when you do that, self-hatred slips in. Self-hatred is the worst type of hatred. In life, people will hate you. Not everyone will like you, and those who do not will reject you. However, some opinions and rejections belong in the trash. The acceptance and love you have for yourself will give you the strength to toss destructive denial into the garbage. However, when self-acceptance and love aren't in place, you cannot throw away fierce criticism. This will mean that you will accept every negative view of everyone who offers one. This is the perfect way to set the ideal stage for self-hate.

Self-hate is so common because there will always be a cause for it. You aren't perfect, and the faults which you possess are evidence of your humanity. These are flaws that should be accepted, even as we try to improve and eliminate them. Defects are not a cause for hatred. Everyone has them, and perfection on this earth is the only thing that does not exist. I once came across a saying that claims that if a plan looks too perfect, it will probably fail. Recognize self-hatred early. Look at the man or woman in the mirror and realize that he or she has worked hard to earn your love. He or she has made some foolish mistakes, but then who hasn't? Do not allow your mistakes to define you. Tell yourself that you are not lazy, sloppy, clumsy, or unintelligent. You may have acted that way, but even Albert Einstein's parents worried that he had a learning disability because when he was young, he was slow to learn to talk. Take inventory of yourself, identify the parts you dislike, accept that they are your flaws, and attempt to fight to improve them while loving yourself every step of the way.

I SEE YOU

Myself and Love

Love is one of the most incredible things in existence. Think about a person who you cannot stand. Maybe their voice is annoyingly high, or they snort when they laugh, or they are overbearing, or their taste in music is awful. Understand that there is someone who looks at that person and loves them. Maybe it is mind-boggling for you. How could anyone stand such a character? Now, realize that it is likely that someone feels the same about you. I grew up with a friend who got on every single nerve I owned. Years later, I watched a gorgeous woman walk down the aisle to marry him, and it shocked me that someone would willingly spend the rest of their life with my annoying friend.

Not that all these people are not flawed. Not that Jennifer doesn't have that annoying voice or that Joe isn't overbearing. Not that you do not have your faults. Instead, the fact is that when love is involved, it makes up for an abundance of flaws.

Do you love yourself? I repeat for emphasis, do you love yourself? I was twenty-one when I first honestly asked myself this question, and the answer almost broke me. I didn't hate myself, but I didn't love myself either. That realization brought on a panic attack (the only one I've ever had), and it felt like my heart was breaking. However, it didn't, and moments later, I had one blatant realization; I *had* to love myself. The only other option was to 'stop living,' and I knew I didn't want that. I realized that I couldn't be superior to others if I weren't nice to myself.

How would there be continuous and unforced niceness in me when I wasn't even nice to me?

Myself and Acceptance

Look in the mirror. Do you see that person there? Ask yourself, "Is this who I am?" Look past the body, look past the flaws, look past the clothes, and look past the physical appearance. Do you see your soul? That's who you are. You can change your outward appearance, but only God can change your soul. Accept that. When an obese person who is unhappy loses weight, they will not attain happiness if their only goal is to change themselves outwardly. If they cannot see the person inside and love that person, it is of little use.

Change Begins with Me

No, it does. *The within affects the without*. The person you are inside will show no matter how hard you try to hide it, just as one cannot conceal smoke from coming forth. So, what happens when you are just not feeling it? Can you trick your mind? No, you cannot fool your mind, but you can change your mind.

The Power of Positive Speaking

Words are powerful. With words, you can build, and you can destroy. Words are like an egg; the moment you let them crack against the walls of an ear, they are heard, and can never be taken back. If everyone tells the most beautiful woman in the world every day that she is ugly, she will believe it, eventually.

If words are so powerful, why not use them to your advantage? Back your actions up with an optimistic speech. Encourage yourself. Look at yourself and call yourself who you want to be.

- ✓ "I am going to do excellent today because I am excellent."

- ✓ "I am going to have a nice day because I am a friendly person."

- ✓ "My mistakes do not define me. I can move past them because I am an overcomer."

Try speaking things like this to yourself multiple times a day and watch them slowly take shape in your life. Avoid using negative or derogatory remarks about yourself. You are royalty, and you deserve more. When you tell yourself continuously that you are no good, you will slowly believe it, and you will act in that manner. Self-talk can be your greatest ally or your greatest nemesis. Which would you instead apply? The choice is yours.

The image you have of yourself is essential. Your self-perception plays an enormous role in how you act and how you treat others. It also affects your attitude. If you have it set in your mind that you will fail, you will give a subpar effort. Because in your mind, the outcome will be the same. Do you see how the way you see yourself carries more weight than you could imagine? The way you see yourself carries more weight than the way others see you. Adjust the view you have of yourself. Until you do that, positive change will remain out of reach. Remember, the change begins with you, the man (woman) in the mirror.

CHAPTER 4

I SEE FRIENDS

"If you live to be 100, I hope I live to be 100 minus 1 day, so I never have to live without you." – **Winnie the Pooh**

The Merriam-Webster Dictionary defines the word friend as, "One attached to another by affection or esteem." Let me make what I consider to be an obvious distinction. This definition isn't talking about social media friends. I've got a little over a thousand of those, and I'm probably on the low end of the "how many friends do you have" scale! I've always felt that a friend cannot indeed be correctly defined. The *word* friend can be determined, but *"a friend"* cannot. Best friend, faithful friend, good friend; we try adjectives to describe what type of friend a person may be, but what makes a person a genuine friend?

31

Maybe it's someone who doesn't lie to you, even when the truth hurts, or perhaps it is someone who will lie to you to preserve your feelings. What makes a person a good friend?

Maybe it is their willingness to go out of their way for you occasionally. Or what makes a person "just a friend?" Is it a person with whom you are acquainted? Well, that would make them (you probably voiced it in your head already) an acquaintance, not a friend, right? I thought Muhammad Ali said it best when he said, "Friendship is the hardest thing in the world to explain. It's not something you learn in school. But if you haven't learned the meaning of friendship, you haven't learned anything."

I'm sure that as you read this, you have your definition of what a friend is to you. More than likely, it is trust, acceptance, willingness to listen, valuing your opinion, and a few other virtues that compel you to stay attached to that person. Most of us probably have at least a few people in our lives that we would call friends, and at least one or two that we would call a best friend. Think of at least one person you would call a "best friend." Think of some things you've been through together; like that time, one of you had to cover for the other one or bail the other person out of a situation. Think of a time you had to cover for someone you might call a friend, but not a best friend. Sometimes, both situations could be similar, and the only difference is that one of those people was your best friend, and the other was "just a friend." The level of friendship doesn't depend on what you do for each other or situations you find yourself in. We might find that it's just the opposite, what you do for that person and what you do with that person, and how you do it depends on the level of friendship.

So, what makes a person your best friend? And what makes a person your friend and not merely an acquaintance? Perhaps only you can answer these questions about what makes a person your friend, and maybe the answer is impossible. One thing seems clear, though, how we view a person plays a part in how we treat that person. Perhaps it shouldn't, but if we're honest with ourselves, it does.

Dr. Daniel Marston is a licensed psychologist specializing in Cognitive Behavioral Therapy, who contends that people do not require intimate relationships like friendships. In an article written for *Psychology Today*, he says, "We need to interact with each other, but it is not necessary that these relationships reach anything more than a basic level of connectedness. It is nice to have strong social relationships but it is not necessary for our survival or even our happiness. Simply put, it is not necessary for humans to have friends."

It's not that I don't think that Dr. Marston has a point about people overemphasizing the importance of social interactions. We must all look in the mirror and decide who we're going to be; no one can tell us that. But I do believe humans must have friends. I think that we are here (existing) to have a relationship with each other. Not that everyone will have a relationship with everyone else, but that we all will have relationships.

The purpose of existence is likely a much bigger subject for another discussion all its own; however, I think we need other people at a very elementary level. I know everyone does not share that belief. Still, if you could imagine for a moment that you have everything you've ever wanted materially, and attained all that you've reached for physically, yet you were the only one on the planet, what would it mean to you? There would be no one to share it with, but you would lack a sense of accomplishment since no one was challenging you. You wouldn't receive any recognition for achievements, and you wouldn't be able to share your thoughts and dreams, and on and on. The fact is, not only do we long for some relationship, but we also need each other for a myriad of reasons. Some of those reasons might even prove to be surprising. Do we need friends to survive? Probably not as friends don't supply oxygen and nutrients. Do we need friends to live? Probably so! Man does not live by bread alone.

In her book, "Friendfluence: the surprising ways friends make us who we are," author Carlin Flora, who was on the staff of *Psychology Today* for eight years, says that evidence suggests that friends have a more significant hand in our development and well-being than do our romantic partners and relatives. She says:

> "More often, the positive influences of friendship are less headline-worthy but still powerful: the daily phone chat and sports betting, the clarifying e-mail from a friend articulating her reservations about your

new boyfriend, or the small unsolicited favor that reminds you during a bleak moment that you are not alone in this world. These gestures are the ones we notice and remember. Meanwhile, such friendships constantly affect us; we've probably never realized-physically and intellectually, and emotionally."

While we all probably define friendship in several ways, perhaps the defining characteristic of friendship is the preference you have for another person. That preference could transcend words and actions that are shared between you and the other person, and cultural boundaries, geographic distance, and values. I look at friendship as a "soup," there are all different from many recipes. However, to have a successful camaraderie or friendships, certain ingredients should be included in this soup. Every friendship doesn't have to have all of these characteristics, but there's a better chance of success if they do. A friendship should include:

- An investment of time.

- Shared emotional support (to some degree).

- A level of vulnerability.

- A certain amount of sacrifice.

- A willingness to apologize (even when you're right), and

- Some common interests.

There may be other ingredients that you could add to the soup, but these are a few.

An ancient Hebrew word for friend is "*oheb*," a participial form meaning "one who loves."
Therefore, we could probably also add loyalty and affection to the ingredients list.

But why is it so important to have friends in your life? It can be a lot of work to maintain the friendship. It's essential because the alternative to having friends in your life would be loneliness.

Yes, we all need to be comfortable in our skin (meaning that we enjoy being with ourselves), but at some point, we all need to interact with other humans. Being lonely for long periods can be a dangerous place to be. Research shows that loneliness can shorten a person's life and erode their health. [16] It may even pose more significant public health risks than smoking. Besides, it can lead to depression. Health coach Grace Jauwena found that:

- 300 million people have depression.

- 16. 2 million adults have experienced a major depressive episode in the past year.

- 10.3 million adults in the U.S. experienced an episode that resulted in severe impairment in the past year.

- Close to 50 percent of all that was diagnosed with depression also diagnosed with an anxiety disorder.

- About 15 percent of the adult population will experience depression at some point in their life.

Although it's challenging to define friendship, part of what makes up a friendship is support, encouragement, and being there in times of need. This may not be a cure for loneliness and depression, but it is medicine. You also realize that while you may consider someone a friend; they may consider you an acquaintance. Which could answer the question, "Why doesn't this person treat me the same way that I treat them?"

The question becomes, how do you view the people in your life? Of all the people you are acquainted with. There are some that you would call a friend. How do you define "a friend" based on those in your life that you contact your friend? How you define that relationship plays a significant part in how you treat those people. You might agree that you should treat everyone with kindness, whether they are your friend or foe. But would you say that you're just a little kinder to the people you call a friend? Would you say that you'd be less likely to jump to a conclusion about someone if they were your friend? In answering these questions, we would also have to factor in those friend descriptions mentioned earlier. Are they a good friend, close friend, best friend? To understand how and why we treat people the way we do, we must determine what they mean to us, and vice-versa. We can't control the way others treat us, but we can control how we treat them. "A man who has friends must himself be friendly..." (Proverbs 18:24)

CHAPTER 5

I SEE PRIVILEGE

"If your White privilege and class privilege protects you, then you have an obligation to use that privilege to take stands that work to end the injustice that grants that privilege in the first place." **- Ayelet Waldman**

The word privilege can be defined as a right or immunity granted as a peculiar benefit, advantage, or favor. In line with that definition, White privilege, societal privilege, and other forms of privilege are unearned advantages or entitlements that are often used to one's benefit at the expense of others. Societal privilege can include age, gender, religion, social class, education level, sexual orientation, and even disability. Privilege is often viewed as something that gives a person an advantage, but what's often missed is that it also puts others at a disadvantage. In her essay "White Privilege: Unpacking the Invisible Knapsack," Peggy McIntosh wrote, "I realized that I had been taught about racism as something that puts others at a disadvantage, but also had been taught not to see one of its corollary aspects, White privilege, which puts me at an advantage."

Often, though, privilege is only associated with wealth, economic status, or family name, though it applies far more broadly. It can be associated with educated people, those perceived to be attractive, ones' position in an organization, skin color within an ethnicity, athletes, entertainers, or even membership in certain religious groups.

Having a conversation about privilege is problematic because, for many people, it causes uncomfortable self-reflection. For example, as a man, I have often acknowledged that women have been, and still are, disadvantaged. In retrospect, though, I can't remember admitting that I am over-privileged because I am a man. Similarly, it's likely that White people, whether inherent or taught, rarely recognize White privilege, in the same way, men do not acknowledge male privilege.

What Privilege is, and What it is not

One reason that many privileged people cannot acknowledge it is because they have a misunderstanding of what it is. In her 2015 article, "Why it's important to think about privilege - and why it's hard," Kathleen Ebbitt, a freelance writer with *Global Citizen* in New York, discusses a conversation she has with a friend regarding privilege. She referenced a *New York Times* article that looked at how high school students thought about privilege. She said, "I find it sad that a student was quoted as saying that she didn't want to be called privileged, just because her parents could buy things." There was a long pause, and my dining companion responded, "Well, who is to say she is privileged?"

She could be experiencing a lot of things that make her life hard. Privilege does not necessarily give a personal exemption from experiencing hardships in their life; privilege does, however, mean that you were extended a right or immunity from liability or duty granted as a particular benefit or advantage. Likewise, White privilege is not the supposition that if you are White, you haven't earned anything you have, nor is it the assumption that White people don't encounter struggle. Many White people do not enjoy the accouterments that accompany White privilege. Peggy McIntosh's article brought out the idea that White privilege is more psychological. White people's lack of awareness has disseminated this subconscious prejudice that they held this power. It can be found in the ability to shop without the fear of being followed or watched, or being confident that your skin color will not work against you when seeking a loan, or not having to have a conversation with your children about school behavior because of your color, or compelling them to go above and beyond to show respect to law enforcement for fear of being hurt or killed.

MICHAEL CARTER

The Conversation Continues

In the U.S. and worldwide, young people of all backgrounds are becoming more and more involved in discussions dealing with race, gender, sexual orientation, religion, culture, and privilege. And while these conversations can be uncomfortable for some, they are not only necessary but paramount to a better social future for people everywhere. We must not discourage the next generation from engaging in these conversations. There is a passage in the Bible in Acts Chapter 17 describes Paul and Silas as those that "have turned the rest of the world upside down, and now they are here disturbing our city." [21] It won't be the next pandemic or financial crisis that will turn the world upside down, I believe it will be the people, and specifically young people, who confront these issues head-on. If the adverse effects of privilege are to be subjugated, those with privilege must tolerate the discomfort of conversations that may cause them to be transparent and self-critical.

The first step toward a better social tomorrow is being taken with the open admission that privilege, and specifically White privilege, exists. I believe that if you want to get where you're going, you must first recognize where you are. With that in mind, if we're going to thrive as a society, we must be realistic about our societal persona. Although recognition, along with admission, is the essential first step, recognition means more than just acknowledging its existence. There must be a genuine, untiring effort to understand the plight of those who are not privileged. In her article "The Silenced Dialogue: Power and Pedagogy in Educating Other People's

I SEE YOU

Children" (Harvard Education Review, Vol. 58, Number 3, August 1988), Lisa Delpit quotes a Black teacher in a multicultural urban elementary school discussing her experiences with her predominately White colleagues about how they should organize reading instruction to best serve the students of color. The teacher says,

> "When you're talking to White people, they still want it to be their way." You can try to talk to them and give them examples, but they're so headstrong, they think they know what's best for everybody, for everybody's children. They won't listen. White folks are going to do what they want to do, anyway. It's really hard. They just don't listen well. No, they listen, but they don't hear – you know how your mama used to say you listen to the radio, but you hear your mother? Well, they don't hear me. So, I just try to shut them out so I can hold my temper. You can only beat your head against a brick wall for so long before you draw blood. If I try to stop arguing with them, I can't help myself from getting angry. Then I end up walking around praying all day. "Please, Lord, remove the bile I feel for those people so I can sleep tonight." It's funny, but it can become cancer, a sore. So, I shut them out. I go back to my little cubby, my classroom, and I try to teach the way I know will work, no matter what those folks say. And when I

43

get Black kids, I just try to undo the damage they did. (pp. 280-281).

A quote like this can be hard to hear; however, if it is not heard and digested, the frustration will remain disguised, and the underprivileged will continue to display malcontent reactions. Does this mean that those who are privileged should be ashamed of it? Since privilege appears to be mostly structural and not individual, being ashamed of it would not be advantageous. The question becomes, what can or should be done about it? The onus falls on those who are privileged. Here are some suggestions to consider:

- Understanding that privilege isn't chosen, but socially given, would be a first step in acknowledging one's privilege.

- Recognizing that one's belief system or value system does not determine privilege can be a significant step. For example, simply because one is opposed to racism or inequality between races or genders does not nullify privilege.

- Identify and seek to change negative behaviors that stem from privilege. Often these behaviors have gone unnoticed because they are ingrained and have become part of who a person is. Egregiously treating those who are not privileged as lazy and unappreciative would be a malicious behavior that comes from privilege.

- Developing a burden for positive change. That burden may come in the form of racial equality, eradicating racism or gender bias, or helping the impoverished live a better life, all while understanding what negative behaviors need to change in you.

- Learn more. Be open to receiving feedback, even if it is hard to hear and hurts a little. What a person does with the input is up to them; however, just being receptive, even if in a small way, helps those who are negatively affected by those with privilege.

These suggestions are not meant to be a collective answer that will solve the problem; however, they can be small steps on a path that leads to a better society for all of us.

CHAPTER 6

I SEE POLITICS

"Reader, suppose you were an idiot. And suppose you were a member of Congress. But I repeat myself."
— **Mark Twain**

I would be lying if I were to say that I didn't have a strong dislike for politics, at least what I perceive to be politics in the modern era. Politics is a multifaceted word, but at its core, politics is a set of activities associated with running a government, state, or area. I am reasonably familiar with a democracy, where the purpose is for citizens to govern themselves either directly or indirectly. The often-quoted words of President Lincoln from the *Gettysburg Address*, that democracy is "...government of the people, by the people, for the people," underlines the term democracy, which comes from the Greek language and means "rule of the people." However, whether you live in a democracy, monarchy, authoritarianism, or one of the many other political systems, you cannot escape politics.

Please don't interpret my dislike for politics as dislike for all politicians, or democracy, which is the political system I am a part of. Instead, my disdain stems from a lack of trust built up over several years in the government to do the right things for all people. Young voters, who will help shape our society's future, are experiencing a trust problem as well. In her article, *Young Voters Know What They Want. But They Don't See Anyone Offering It*, *New York Times* political reporter Maggie Astor says, "For the first time, millennials and Generation Z have enough electoral clout to compete with their elders seriously. But many feel more disillusioned than empowered."

Perhaps, as with many in my generation, their disappointment stems from the failed expectations of government leaders to help structure the future in a way that benefits the people. Instead, comparison, character assassination, defamation, and dirty politics are what they mostly see, while the desire for social justice, equality, healthcare, and other issues are pushed to the back burner. Of the people who I had conversations with in researching this book, about eighty percent were millennials or Gen-Z. And what I found is that they are more passionate about issues than they are about institutions. Young people care about social problems and are in favor of the greater good over partisan politicking. Unlike any previous generation, young people share the same issues as people that don't look like them or come from the same background that they do. Consequently, their political stances are greatly affected as a result of the overabundance of shared concerns.

Need for Political Involvement

Plato said, "One of the penalties for refusing to participate in politics is that your inferiors will eventually govern you."

A cursory look at our society, both in government and in the functioning of our many institutions, shows the rise of mediocrity, with the best and brightest terrified either by the hatred of our politics, fear of the political crisis or loss of interest, trust and belief in our democratic system and mechanism.

In the very sporadic instances where any disillusioned and disaffected voiced their complaints and somewhat muffled reprimanding remarks, they are viewed with a dismissiveness that is filled with denial, often outright hatred and indifference. What we see in the international room is a growing debt burden, economic stagnation, social turmoil, rising ethnic tensions, increasing inequality, increasing religious extremism, etc. It is therefore regrettable that many of us still sit on the sidelines or are ensconced in our silos of political apathy and indifference in the face of such national malaise.

This is now maybe the time to distinguish between political participation and political activity. Although political involvement could include financial donations to campaigns or political parties, voting, campaign organizing, and even contacting officeholders, political participation could take the form of participating in any action that forms influences the democratic process or outcomes, such as attending party conventions and registering. It can be said that there is not much of a distinction between the two. Studies in political science inform us that one of the fundamental civic responsibilities of any citizenry is to participate in the political system and process, whether they vote for a candidate seeking political office, take part in acts of peaceful civil protest or communicate their opinions and beliefs.

It is my honest opinion that we, as citizens, can do so much to change our society's governance trajectory if we can only resolve to get actively involved rather than leave the political process to grafters and political charlatans. As we all know, and as I discover, every act of political conquest results in the conqueror imposing his views, vision, objectives, and values on the conquered. We have allowed ourselves to be part of the conquered and oppressed majority by staying away from any form of political involvement despite our positions in society, level of affluence, or education. Whether or not we like it, we all have invisible scars of the political system and process which some privileged few have exploited and seized.

It's time to face the fact that there's no perfect life or an ideal world, so it's our responsibility as decent people not to be political observers but to get interested in creating a new age of politics and leadership in which we can disagree with each other and stay friends we pursue common ground and consensus with openness and modesty. Much of the time, people in our living situations seem to forget that we are animals before we are prey. We separate ourselves from happenings beyond our cocoon of comfortability because we find ourselves protected and unaffected by policy outcomes that affect others. Most of them suffer from severe cases of dissociation, separating ourselves from ourselves before we are victims. Conscious of the fact that all things of lasting importance require a great effort and dedication and not a result of convenience, it was a source of eternal consolation to understand that today's struggles offer rise to the glory of tomorrow and that the agony and sorrow of realizing that at one stage in our lives we had the potential to bring about progress in the lives of others. As Apple's co-founder

I SEE YOU

Ronald Wayne said, "The future belongs to those who can foresee it and give everything they need to get there."

I must confess that few of us consider our impact on the future of our society and how to influence it, or better still, see the possibilities of a glorious future and work diligently towards its realization. No country is more significant than its culture, its institutions, and its constitution, and to the degree that we strive to a better nation, let us not only make fame with our accomplishments and victories but use that fame to improve the lives of people.

Let's have hope-hope that looks through the uncertainty of the moment and the possibility of the future because the government has no self-correcting process unless we can move it in the right direction. So, I want to encourage any political observer to get involved in politics because what they are running out of, they can run into those who believe that the walls of our political process and action are too tight to break; let them remember that even the most hardened wall can crumble because all that's needed is to find a crack on its surface.

German theater practitioner, playwright, and poet Bertolt Brecht once said, "The worst illiterate is the political illiterate. He hears nothing, sees nothing, takes no part in political life. He doesn't seem to know that the cost of living, the price of beans, of flour, of rent, of medicines all, depends on political decisions. He even prides himself on his political ignorance, sticks out his chest, and says he hates politics. The imbecile doesn't know that from his political non-participation comes the prostitute, the abandoned child, the robber and, worst of all, corrupt officials, the lackeys of exploitative multinational corporations."

Martin Luther King, Jr.

DR. MARTIN LUTHER KING JR., the undisputed leader of the nonviolent Civil Rights Movement in the 1960s, was also one of the most admired and despised men of his time. King's promise of reform by peaceful means contributed to the numbers of the movement from his participation in the Montgomery bus boycott in 1955 to his untimely death in 1968 and gave it its moral strength. Martin Luther King Jr.'s legacy is expressed in these two simple terms: dignity and nonviolence.

King was brought up in an activist family. In the 1920s, his father was deeply influenced by the BACK TO AFRICA MOVEMENT by Marcus Garvey. His mother was the daughter of one of the most prominent African American ministers in Atlanta. King excelled as a student. He surpassed his classmates in school, and at fifteen, attended Morehouse College, his father's alma mater. He then attended Crozer Theological Seminary, where he was awarded a Bachelor of Divinity. He met and married CORETTA SCOTT while earning his doctorate at Boston University. King accepted an invitation to the Dexter Street Baptist Church in Montgomery, Alabama, after earning his Ph.D. in 1955.

King founded the Southern Christian Leadership Conference after his leadership of the bus boycott, which promoted African Americans' rights. In April 1963, King organized a rally in Birmingham, Alabama, a city king called "the most profoundly segregated city in the United States." Sixty unsolved bombings of African American churches and homes had occurred since the end of World War II.

They organized boycotts, sit-ins, and marches. As Birmingham Police Department Chief Bull Connor used fire hoses and dogs on the protesters, millions watched the altercations on TV. They arrested King several times. Yet support for King and his family came from across the nation and around the world. He then delivered his famous address, "I Have a Dream," to thousands in Washington, D.C., in 1963.

King turned his attempts to educate African American voters in the south following the 1964 Civil Rights Act. In 1965 he led a march to lift the number of African American voters in Alabama in Selma, Alabama. King was charged yet again. The marchers also witnessed police violence. Tear gas, cow prods, and billy clubs struck the unarmed protesters. Popular sentiment overwhelmingly supported King and the demonstrators. Finally, President Johnson ordered the National Guard to guard the demonstrators, and King could complete the long march from Selma to the Montgomery state capital. The Selma action led to the passage of the 1965 Voting Rights Act.

James Earl Ray assassinated King early on the morning of April 4, 1968. Spontaneous violence spread through urban areas as mourners expressed their anger at the death of their leader. Many American cities are breaking into anarchy.

It is also remarkable that the community never ignored his achievements. In 1963 *Time Magazine* named him "Man of the Year." He received the Nobel Peace Prize in 1964 and was described as "The first human in the Western World to convince us that a fight can be fought without violence." He was awarded the Presidential Medal of Freedom posthumously in 1977, the highest honor a civilian American could receive. His birthday, January 15, became a national holiday in the 1980s, providing a yearly chance for Americans to focus on the two values he devoted his life to advertising.

I SEE YOU

Martin Luther King Jr was one of many non-politicians who changed the world by being actively involved. How you see politics undoubtedly affects your willingness to be involved in it.

CHAPTER 7

I SEE MULTICULTURAL

"We become not a melting pot but a beautiful mosaic. Different people, different beliefs, different yearnings, different hopes, different dreams." **- Jimmy Carter**

In one of my high school science classes some time ago, we explored "water." The teacher asked us a question that sparked a heated debate. She wondered, *is water colorless*? Each person stood up one after another, with confidence, and answered the question. Almost everyone claimed that water is colorless except for a few classmates who argued that water is white. We argued over the color of water throughout the class period and even continued at lunch. The next time we met, our teacher came to class with a bottle filled with water and transparent glass. "Class, we are doing something interesting today," she said with a serious yet playful look.

I SEE YOU

We all watched her as she gently uncovered the bottle filled with water. Before she poured the water into a jar, she asked a question that sparked another debate. She asked, "Is water tasteless?"

We all laughed. What kind of problem is that? Water is tasteless. We assumed that this was a trick question, or she just didn't think we were bright. Water is tasteless! Some of us made sarcastic comments, and others laughed. Amid the noise, she found her way to calm the class. She asked again, "Is water colorless?" She knew by now that we figured that there must be more to the question.

Naturally, water appears to be tasteless, but what about salty beach water? We say it is salty, right? The saltiness makes the beach water different from freshwater. We have fish like bluefish, cod, halibut, tuna, and others that can only survive in saltwater but can't survive in freshwater. There are fish such as salmon, eels, red drums, and many others living in freshwater, but they cannot survive in saltwater. Then, some fish can survive in saltwater and freshwater equally. Every fish is unique, regardless of the water or the environment it lives in.

What if we say that water is colorless? What do we say about the water from the blue sea? We say it is colorful, right? The answers to these questions are different depending on individual views.

Like the discussion about water, still today, we have many unresolved views on matters regarding humanity in which multicultural is one. As long as humanity has existed, the question has been which culture is superior? Throughout history, there have been various attempts to integrate all cultures. One example was from the 4th century B.C. when Alexander the Great was conquering. He was spreading Greek culture, and he wanted everyone to be Grecian. This process of cultural change was called Hellenization. The idea was to establish a unique culture among diverse people. To be a Hellenists meant that you adopted the ways of the Greek culture, and you also spoke Greek. So, you might be Jewish, and you might be Italian or something else. But Alexander the Great wanted to get everyone on the same page culturally. Some Jews embraced Hellenization, but others who were more orthodox did not. The ones that did not were called Hebrews.

Most everyone defends their own culture, and the fear of being dominated by another culture scares them. Just like everyone tried to assert their point in the science class, they see their point as the correct view. Similarly, people try to protect their culture and preserve it to be passed down to future generations.

The simplest definition you can give culture is that; it is the way of life of a specific group of people. Life could be language, dress, food, political system, religion, beliefs, and other ideologies. A society can contain over one culture or ethnic group. Therefore, we say that such a society is multicultural. We have different people with different cultures in workplaces, families, schools, hospitals, and places of business.

I SEE YOU

Multiculturalism is a word that describes a society where many cultures live together, and each culture is respected as much as any other one. In my experience, multiculturalism has sometimes been confused with being multiracial. I've visited several "mega-churches" over the past three decades, and most have been predominately White. One thing most of them had in common, whether being mostly White, Black, or another race, is that many of them portrayed the mantra of being multicultural. However, when I take a more in-depth look at the makeup of the church, I see that in predominately White churches, most of the music is a particular genre, most, if not all the leaders are White, the art, décor, and small groups mostly emanate one specific culture. In the churches I visited that were primarily Black, I found the same thing. And although I didn't see that projecting a particular culture to be a bad thing, it just appeared that calling it multicultural when they meant multiracial is an oversight.

People and Culture

People travel the world for many reasons, and one benefit could be to learn about new cultures. An American traveling to Asia intending to spend any significant time there will have to learn something about the Asian culture if he or she wants to enjoy his or her stay.

I have a friend who told me the story of a man who visited twenty-five countries. He learned as much as he could about their languages, foods, and many other things. In many of those countries, he conducted business.

On one of his visits to a particular country, to his surprise, a family "gifted" a beautiful young lady to him to marry. This culture believed the best gift they could give him in appreciation for his kindness was a young lady. It was difficult for him to accept this "gift" not because she was unattractive, but because his culture demanded that love exists between two people *before* they marry, and that marriage was to be consensual. Love is foundational to marriage in most cultures, but that is not the case in this culture. In their culture, polygamy is not a problem, but it is an abomination in the traveler's culture. In this host culture, they believe that love is not an essential ingredient to a marriage. Almost all the men in the society had over one wife, and the number of wives they had assessed their wealth. Women were an object for sex and reproduction. A woman who cannot conceive and have a child is labeled a witch. In the travelers' culture, they practice the direct opposite of this host society's culture. A relationship between two people should only result in marriage if both people find love for each other. This culture was strange and unacceptable to this American traveler, the same way it would be odd to anyone who holds different cultural beliefs from theirs.

He could not reconcile his cultural beliefs with this host society. And because of this cultural conflict, in his mind, he thought changing their culture to his own was the best solution.

He began the campaign, preaching and persuading with the help of some young folks who loved him. Some embraced his culture, but they still had their culture in

60

their blood. Many rejected his culture, and they despised him for wanting to change them. He tried bribing them with money and gifts from his home country, and some people found his kindness attractive. But they didn't throw away their own culture. They had conserved their culture deep in their hearts. The ones who detested the new culture and never wanted to embrace it were forced to embrace it against their will.

The man was satisfied, and he felt that he had coaxed the people into leaving their own culture. He believed he had succeeded, but the people who were forced to adapt to his culture eventually brought back their culture from its hidden place in their hearts. They dusted it off like an old book from the bookshelf. However, because of the different levels at which the people adopted the foreign culture, it was not as it used to be; this new culture was adulterated. They did their best to find a way to balance the foreign culture and their indigenous culture. As they were exposed to different cultures from different visitors, they learned how to find symmetry between foreign cultures and their indigenous culture. Their society became multicultural, but it has many open to cultural conflicts.

The world itself is multicultural. We can't but help to accept this reality. Many people, however, are like this traveler. They look down on other people's cultures because they are covered with an assumption of human cultural superiority.

MICHAEL CARTER

Multiculturalism within a person is defined as the degree to which they know, identify with, and internalize more than one culture. According to the *Oxford English Dictionary 8th Edition*, multiculturalism is defined as "the practice of giving importance to all cultures."

We have a multicultural society today because people move from one place to another like nomadic herdsmen. Immigration has occurred throughout history, and people have been moving from their native habitats for various reasons.

Looking back at history, by the early 1600s, the U.S. Eastern Seaboard was sprinkled with European immigrants, including the Spanish in Florida, the British in New England and Virginia, the Dutch in New York, and the Swedes in Delaware. The first Africans landed in North America and the territory that would become the United States, thousands of years before Europeans crossed the vast Atlantic by ship and settlement en masse. During the last Ice Age, they were Native American ancestors who crossed a narrow spit of land linking Asia to North America some 20,000 years ago. These are people with different languages, different religions, different thoughts, different beliefs, different ideologies of life, and other histories.

Today migration is still taking place worldwide; people leave one country for another intending to settle and make a living in that country permanently. People migrate to other countries for different reasons, the most common being to gain a better standard of living. People became multicultural individuals as they move from one country to another due to war, marriage, education acquisition, missionary work, healthy living, adventure, politics, and many other things. In 2006, Canada's population statistics reported that they received 236,756 immigrants. The top ten countries of origin were China (28,896), India (28,520), Philippines (19,718), Pakistan (9,808), United States (8,750), UK (7,324), Iran (7,195), South Korea (5909), Colombia (5,382), Sri Lanka (4,068), France (4,026), Morocco (4,025), Romania, Russia and Algeria each contributing over 3,000 immigrants.

Imagine a scenario where there is a mixture of people of a different color, social exposure, and mindsets all in a meeting to deliberate the subject of arranged marriages. They would likely never reach a compromise on this issue, and that may not be such a bad thing. It is the result of cultural differences at play. Short of immorality and injustice, some things are probably better left to the people; otherwise, it opens the door for breaching cultural respect.

What has Failed?

"This multicultural approach, saying that we live side by side and live happily with each other, has failed. Utterly failed." Angela Merkel.

Two years ago, two people were joined in holy matrimony. Both imagined a bright future in their new home with their new life. They had both fantasized about how beautiful their new journey would look. Although they accepted advice from counselors, parents, and pastors, cultural issues eventually surfaced, and a consensus seemed impossible. Topics like child discipline, finances, politics, religion; perhaps they forgot that they were from different backgrounds. The union did not take too long before it went sour. The more they couldn't agree, the more pain, hatred, disloyalty, bitterness, and aggression toward each other increased. Although they are still together, not willing to compromise on cultural issues keeps strife in the marriage. What a life they live.

Remarkably they appear different in public. Holding hands, kissing, hugging, and exchanging pleasant compliments with the aura of love gained them social acceptance. Everyone who knew them wanted their own love life to be like theirs, not knowing that this model couple was not what they appeared to be. The couple finally realized that they needed help. Their journey to seek help began. They accepted the fact that they needed serious relationship counseling. Although the counseling was successful, it took them years of deliberate hard work to get each other and form their own new family culture. In every corner of their home, they posted the mantra, *"Our pretense can become real only if we are intentional about it,"* which fueled their journey to a successful marriage.

Just like this couple, the world at large has adopted a pretense for a long time. The White, the Black, the brown, the red, and many other colors have long lived in this pretense. It's of little wonder that they find it easy to ignite the fire of hatred whenever the opportunity arises. Most everyone, if not all, has experienced discrimination in their life based on their social culture, political culture, family culture, or individual culture. To think there should be an integrated lifestyle for all different cultures, and not just side by side, sounds like an impossibility. We treat other people of a different culture, cause them to ask, "What is wrong with my culture?" and subsequently feel inferior as a people. In schools, they should design the curriculum to accommodate multiculturalism through history and current events, but in a genuine sense, we don't see true multiculturalism.

Some schools make matters worse because they discriminate against different cultures. They kept Black children at one table while the White children were at another table eating lunch. A teacher once shared her experience in dealing with children of different races and colors. She confessed that children do better in learning in school if they have a good number of other children that share their culture. I pondered her confession for some time, and it hurts my heart to think children are powerless in the way they are programmed. I asked, "Why does a child do better when she is among other children who share the same culture with her? What makes learning among other children from other cultures different? Are teachers biased in their assessment of the children from a minority culture? What are the parents saying to the children concerning others with different cultures? Are the parents sincere? What is society teaching the children?

MICHAEL CARTER

In the UK, they have the very definition of a multicultural society, much the same (almost) as the USA and Australia. I've heard it said, though, that multiculturalism encourages racism. But like many other things, it's not multiculturalism that promotes racism, and it's the heart of a person and how they perceive someone, not like them. I remember being asked, "Is America a melting pot or a salad bowl?" My reply is, "Yes!" These cultures all co-exist as one while maintaining their characteristics (salad bowl). Therefore, racism in America does not stem from multiculturalism; in part, it stems from a fear of losing power.

When you juxtapose multiculturalism with the reality that a melting pot is not fostering harmony, issues of segregation and integration arise.

Segregation occurs when you reject those that differ from you; integration occurs when you include those that are different because you see the similarities behind the apparent differences. Which group do you belong to? Is it the segregation group or integration group?
The beauty of humanity lies in the different ethnicities; diversity enriches your life with learning opportunities, rather than threatening your identity.

For a long time, people have introduced different policies to accommodate and build a multicultural society. A multicultural society where no one feels inferior and every culture is unique. No matter the approach that may be adapted, to accommodate all cultures without the individual efforts to make it work, it is just useless.

I SEE YOU

An Asset

When a society is open to multiculturalism, the individuals in that society develop identification with over one culture. This can help facilitate connections with others and build strong relationships among diverse cultures. Identification with over one culture can help reduce connections with others. There is no problem with internalizing more than one culture; the issue is that our perception about those that look, and act differently than us has restricted our ability to understand and accept them.

There are problems when individuals decide that their culture is the only valid one. There are problems when small groups can't live in the present and release the bonds from the past. There are problems when cultures try to make their culture dominant by changing the rules and laws. The problem isn't multiculturalism. The problem lies with the perception held by those people, groups, and cultures.

"Multiculturalism is a good reminder that when standards are relative, there are no standards." Victor Davis Hanson.

If everyone looks the same, eats the same, thinks the same, believes the same, and cheers for the same team, don't you think the world will be boring?

The world is enormous enough to accommodate all cultures, as the sky is vast enough for all birds to fly. Birds don't struggle for space in the sky, so why should humans work with one another. The differences we possess should be to keep us together as one. If there are no different cultures, will there ever be a place to see new things? We should abandon thoughts on the supremacy of one culture over another. No one, no culture, no race, and no ethnicity is supreme.

By going deeper into relationships and social interactions, you can foster unity within diversity; by discussing values and creating intimacy. You don't have to be friends with everyone, and you don't even have to be friends with those who think the same way you do.

A good friend of mine once argued that cultures are not equal. He backed up his point by claiming that African cultures allow girls' mistreatment and the act of rape by blaming the victim. On the surface, American culture does not condone or accept this behavior against women and girls.

To my friend, this makes the American culture supreme. The good news is no culture is supreme over the other. American culture encourages abortion, but African culture doesn't tolerate abortion.

Should Africans now say their culture is supreme over American culture because of that? We all need different thoughts, values, and standards to keep moving. If we want peace, we can create it; if we want equality, we can also make it. Even if its war, we can create it; it all depends on our perceptions. There are flaws in every culture, but instead of cultural assimilation or appropriation, sharing values would go a long way toward multicultural harmony.

Let's train our minds to embrace the good; let's train our minds to be positive. We should blame no individual or group for their circumstances or behavior; they should not be seen as unfortunate; neither should they be made to pay for the consequences of wars in the past. Except for immorality, there is no behavior they need to change, and they just need to be accepted. If you need change at all, then it lives in our ability to accommodate others truly. If we have not seen the right time to purge our minds of negative thoughts about other people's cultures, I think it is high time to purify our minds and keep it clean.

If you want to promote tolerance of diversity, start by acknowledging your contradictions. Until you can begin embracing others, you must become conscious of yourself. Because of our ingrained perceptions, it will take time for this to actualize.

"It is not our differences that divide us. We cannot recognize, accept, and celebrate those differences." Audre Lorde.

CHAPTER 8

I SEE RELIGION

"Religion is the clearest telescope through which we can behold the beauties of creation." **Williams Scott Downey**

Religion has been defined in the dictionary as, "...the belief in and worship of superhuman controlling power, especially a personal God or gods." The term religion has been used extensively throughout the world. Almost everyone has a belief in a higher power. In the London based news magazine, *The Guardian Weekly*, one article says that "Faith is on the rise and 84% of the global population identifies with a religious group" (Sherwood, Harriet). Just like culture differs, religions differ in the same way. According to that same article, as of 2015, "Christians form the biggest religious group by some margin, with 2.3 billion adherents or 31.2% of the total world population of 7.3 billion. Next come Muslims (1.8

billion, or 24.1%), Hindus (1.1 billion, or 15.1%) and Buddhists (500 million, or 6.9%)." Teachings in different religions vary, and those teachings have a direct effect on how people that follow them think. Each religion has its value and belief system. That belief system can primarily affect a person's view of how life should be lived.

For example, someone may believe that eating an apple is terrible because Adam and Eve ate an apple, which resulted in their banishment from the Garden of Eden. To some, that may sound ridiculous, right? I mean, how on Earth can someone detest eating an apple because of its role in history; it wasn't the apple that caused their banishment, and it was their disobedience.

Another example would be how Christians call God "Father." According to the Bible, those who believe in God are called children of the Father. **1 John 3:1 (NIV).** However, of the 99 names ascribed to God in Islam, "Father" is omitted to avoid the Father and Son (Jesus). This is in stark contrast to the Bible and Jesus' teaching.

Undoubtedly, there is religious freedom, and no one should be mistreated or abused because of religious differences. If a person wants to show often, religious beliefs are transferred from the parents to the children. Most times, the children do not choose their religion; they only imbibe their parents' thoughts. A child rarely practices a different belief from that of his or her parent.

As a Christian growing up, I was exposed to other religions. I mixed with other children who held different religious beliefs, and I admired their views, ways of worship, and dress. Once I got home, I would try to practice some things I saw them doing. I would ask my mother to buy me a rosary. It was only admiration, and because of my environment, I would never have gone beyond that.

My mom, who not only brought me into the world but also influenced my worldview, was a churchgoer. Until I reached a certain age, I had no choice other than embracing her beliefs. The teachings of religious beliefs and ideologies start from childhood. By the time the child becomes an adult, they would have assimilated those teachings and apply them along their journey, or at some point, choose to follow a different path based on many factors, including exposure, education, and experience. By the way, many people do not believe in religion. Atheists, who do not believe in a supernatural God or are somewhere out there, believe that the world exists without a supernatural influence. Agnostics believe that nothing is known or can be known of the existence or nature of God or anything beyond material phenomena. An unbeliever would neither claim belief nor disbelief in God.

Today there are some 4,300 world religions. Determining the actual number of religions in the world may be difficult because some religions have just a few people practicing them.

It is also restricted by territory. Before researching it, I was only aware of a few religions.

I SEE YOU

Through research, I found out there are more than 4000 religions globally; that's amazing.

To mention a few, Christianity, Islam, Hinduism, Buddhism, Chinese traditional religions, Primal indigenous, African traditional religions, Sikhism, Juche, Spiritism, Judaism, Bahai, Jainism, Shirito, Cao Dai, Zoroastrianism, Tenrikyo, Neopaganism, and Unitarian Universalism. We can say that there is extensive diversity in people's beliefs. I also found that one thing common in most countries is that there must be a religion/religious belief that dominates the country.

In Iraq, for example, it is the Islamic religion that dominates. In Nigeria, Christianity and Islam are the most common. In China, you find that Buddhism is most prevalent. The Indian subcontinent is the birthplace of four of the world's major religions, namely Hinduism, Buddhism, Jainism, and Sikhism.

Let's place it on the table; let's assume that we have 3000 workers in a company, each of them following a different religion with different beliefs. Still, they all have an equilibrium on morality, or perhaps they don't have any stability on a character. One thousand employees might have been exposed to the teaching that murder and suicide are not only permissible but necessary. The other 2000 workers have imbibed the teaching that murder and suicide are sins according to their beliefs. I presume that unity in such a place has about a 50-50 chance of survival. The people from the first group may decide that they will kill those of the second group that refuses to share their beliefs. Perhaps those in the second group are left at the mercy of those in the first group for fear of being killed.

That company is a microcosm of the world in a genuine sense. Imagine the profound chasm that exists because so-called religions in the world have such varying different beliefs.

Religion and the World

In the past, the world has witnessed several religious conflicts at different times in different countries. The disputes were inter-religion or intra-religion. It is not new to say that even people of the same belief still struggle in conflict. It is certainly not unusual to see people who receive the same teachings and believe in the same "superpower" struggle to share common ground. It happens all over the place. Religious conflict in America is as old as America itself. America has experienced both inter-religious and intra-religious conflict.

Many religions teach that their followers should both evangelize and live in a way that would persuade others to join them. However, when followers of religion try to obtrude their religious beliefs on others, it results in contentious religious conflict most of the time. For example, a Muslim may be prohibited from drinking alcohol or eating pork, but Islam has no closeness to the strict limits on what Orthodox Jews can and cannot do on the Sabbath. Because of its idea of reincarnation, Hinduism falls somewhat into this category and believes that behavior in this life will affect the next. Because these beliefs are deeply rooted, forcing one's opinions on another will only drive a more substantial wedge between believers.

When the policies or laws designed by governmental bodies disagree with the core beliefs of a religion, it will surely attract criticism and opposition from the affected religious bodies. When abortion was legalized, there was a protest by the Christians in the US. A similar thing happened when same-sex marriage was legally approved. When the core beliefs that define a religious groups' identity are challenged, they felt the need to respond to the encroachment on their religious beliefs. But because of this, they view Christians as close-minded radicals who are out of touch with the times. Religious beliefs unquestionably affect our perception of others, especially those who hold a different faith.

Maybe we should take a moment and reflect on how the religion we practice has affected our relationship with the world and how it has affected our personal lives? How has it affected politics? How has it affected the world at large?

Sometimes I try to engage people in discussions centered on religion. I want to know how their religious beliefs affect their thought process. I want to know how they treat people who hold different views than their core beliefs. I found out that each follower of a particular religion desperately wants to protect their faith. If the teachings of religion are rooted and grounded in the follower's mind, it would seem that an argumentative, contentious debate would yield no fruit.

Religious beliefs are essential, however. For example, if two people fall in love and get married, they must center on their premarital discussions on religious beliefs. If one's religious beliefs are polytheistic (the belief in many gods), and the other's religion is monotheistic, will they teach their children? Can their relationship grow in harmony when their faith in the supernatural is so disparate? In this case, if they can't agree, the worst that should happen is that they decide not to get married. Religious beliefs go far beyond marriage decisions, though. How a person worships and what they believe about the supernatural can affect how they are viewed, which will affect the way they are treated. Fellowship and friendship with someone who thinks differently than you may not be possible; however, discrimination should not be the answer.

"It is important to understand discrimination based on a person's religion or lack of thereof is legally equivalent to discriminating against a person because of his or her race." Jeff Seaver.

A friend of mine visited another country to celebrate his fourth wedding anniversary with his wife. The country is attractive to tourists because of its beauty and its advances in technology. The environment, the tourist guide, and everyone they met were amiable. On one of their visits to the beach, he was sitting with his wife, enjoying the cool breeze, the beautiful scenery, and other tourists. As he was relaxing, the thought came to him that this would be a beautiful place to live and work. Although he was doing well in his career at home, he felt the need for a new adventure, and possibly another country. After returning to the states, he thought more about it, talked it over with his wife, and moved to this country where he felt he could excel even more in his career. He applied for a job and could get a well-paid position in one of the country's most prominent technology firms. Things were happening so fast as he uprooted his family and moved. That was a new beginning for him and his family. He worked with pure honesty and diligence. He dedicated his time to his new job wholeheartedly, but as (I removed he should I keep the original word?) time went on, he was not rewarded for it. He felt as though he was being ostracized and even discriminated against. His coworkers were not impressed with his work even though, in his estimation, it was exceptional. After working tirelessly for four years, they denied him a promotion he knew he was the most qualified to get.

Some employees who started working at the company after he did were granted a promotion after two years. He thought the management had possibly forgotten to add him to their eligibility for the promotion list. He finally questioned his employer about why he was being overlooked. The reply was merely one sentence.

"We are sorry the promotion position is meant for............ religious member."

He realized that it was not because he was a foreigner, they overlooked him, but because of his religious views. His only two options were to quit the job he loved or embrace the mantra, "If you can't beat them, join them."

That story gives a picture of clear discrimination based on religion. In the world today, the level of discrimination on the grounds of religion is alarming. When a person does not, it is crucial to others' religious beliefs; they see the person as an antagonist. Sometimes, even as a threat.

Often, a religious follower tries to coerce people into their religion through the use of force. Others try to be diplomatic about it, but whatever the method, choice of religion remains a right that all humans share.

During the Abyssinia–Somalia war, which started as military, the leader Imam Ahmed Ibn Ibrahim Al- Ghazi forcibly converted all of its survivors to Islam. Another is the Sudanese civil war from 1983 to 2005, where the Muslim central government attempted to impose sharia law on all non-Muslim followers. This resulted in the separation of Sudan and South Sudan. The Muslims occupy Sudan while the Christians have their space in South Sudan.

It is said that some religions, which supposedly espouse peace, love, and harmony, are so commonly connected with intolerance, aggression, and hatred.

I am not diminishing the impact of religion on people, society, and the world. Many religious beliefs and their teachings have helped to achieve some levels of morality and decency. For example, as a Christian, I find it difficult to steal from someone instead of working and giving because I have assimilated the Bible's teaching on stealing. Ephesians 4:28 (NIV).

Meanwhile, religion has helped to create fear in some people to do the right thing. People are afraid, scared of doing something against their religion, or not doing something for their faith. Thus, religion is often blamed for terrible acts that people commit. Humans are to be blamed, not necessarily a religion; religion does not create fear humans do; religion does not kill, humans do, religion does not discriminate, the human does. We all have a choice and can decide whether to follow the tenets of faith. But here lies the problem, doesn't it? Choice. If a human has to search for morality, that will mean they don't possess it already. So how can one make a choice in which religion is right?

"Religion is never the problem: it's the people who use it to gain power." Julian Casablanca.

"If your religion requires you to hate someone. It would be best if you had a new religion." Anonymous.

Personal Religion

If you must, please skip the last part of this chapter, as it is not my intention (in this book) to bloviate my personal religious beliefs. However, as a Christian pastor, I would be remiss if I didn't promulgate where I stand.

What religion can be termed true religion? Is it Christianity? Is it Islam? Is it Jewish? Or is it Buddhist? The fundamental problem with religion today is that everyone tries to convince another that their faith is the true religion. Every religious group follower wants to show to the world how true and magnificent they are.

"We have enough religion to make us hate, but not enough to make us love one another." Thomas Jefferson.

I am a Christian. The dictionary defines Christianity as the religion derived from Jesus Christ, based on the Bible as sacred scripture, and professed by Eastern, Roman Catholic, and Protestant bodies.[26] Mostly, I agree with that definition, with one glaring conflict. I cannot define Christianity as a religion. Not because I believe the dictionary definition of religion is grossly errant. Still, the word religion, too many, implies a set of rules, blind faith, infallible traditions, and performing good deeds to get into Heaven or "the Good Place" in the afterlife. Christianity, however, is based on a *relationship* with Jesus. Undoubtedly many profess to be Christian, yet don't act as though they are. And people judge Christianity based on those actions.

Christianity itself does not discriminate. If you are human, you can be a Christian. There is one way, and one way only, to believe that Jesus Christ died on the cross and that God raised Him from the dead. That's it. No amount of works or lack thereof will gain you access to Heaven apart from this belief. Besides, if you hate, discriminate, or look down on anyone else because of your faith, you're doing it wrong.

I SEE YOU

"Religion is the mortar that binds society: the granite pedestal of liberty; the strong backbone of the social system." Thomas Guthrie.

If religion binds the world together, then we must outgrow criticizing one another based on faith. Any religion that oppresses or persecutes will find it challenging to convince others it is accurate and right. One reason I love Christianity is that it chases after potential converts with love, even if some who claim to be Christians do not. It's a pity that humans put themselves in bondage by hating one another.

Religion is not the problem; how we perceive each other based on religion is the problem.

CHAPTER 9
I SEE TOLERANCE

"If a man is to survive, he will have learned to delight in the essential differences between men and between cultures. He will learn that differences in ideas and attitudes are a delight, part of life's exciting variety, not fear." — **Gene Roddenberry**

Tolerance can be described as the ability to accept diversity, live, and let others live. It is the act of continuing activities not relevant to you or of which you disapprove. A person with a high quotient of tolerance could exercise fair and aim behavior towards those whose opinions differ from his.

You accept and learn from others by being inclusive, valuing differences, bridging cultural divides, challenging unfair assumptions, finding common ground, and creating new ties. Tolerance is the opposite of prejudice.

I SEE YOU

Tolerance is, in my mind, essential to a healthy life. Tolerance means treating others just the way you want to be treated. We live in a world that is a potpourri of cultural traditions, which leads to meaningful differences between people. As individuals, we are expected to communicate with people of different cultures, ethnicities, nationalities, races, and religions. The surrounding diversity reflects our circle of friends, schoolmates, college-mates, colleagues in the office, and all the surrounding people. In short, progress in today's world depends on appreciating others' work and respecting each other's differences.

For a genuine appreciation of the meaning of tolerance, there must be a deep understanding of intolerance and discrimination, for those are the twin demons which tolerance seeks to overcome

Intolerance and Discrimination

Discrimination in all its different ways and words-is one of the most prevalent forms of prejudice and exploitation of human rights. Each day it affects millions of people and is one of the hardest to recognize. Do you realize it?

Discrimination and intolerance are concepts that are closely related. Intolerance denotes a lack of regard for other beliefs or creeds besides one's own. This means excluding people we view as different from us, like members of a racial or cultural group other than our own, or people of different political or sexual orientation. Intolerance can manifest in the form of avoidance, hate speech, physical injury, or even murder.

MICHAEL CARTER

Discrimination happens when individuals are viewed less fairly than others because they belong to or are belonging to a specific community or category. Persons may be discriminated against on account of age, disability, nationality, origin, political ideology, race, faith, gender, sexual identity, language, culture, and other reasons.

Discrimination, which is often the product of prejudiced conclusions, renders people helpless, prohibits them from being productive citizens, keeps them from improving their talents, and, in some instances, getting jobs, health care, education, or accommodation.
Discrimination directly impacts individuals or communities being discriminated against and has indirect and significant implications for society. A society where racism is permitted or tolerated is a society in which people are deprived of the freedom to exercise their full potential for themselves and the community.

Structural Discriminations

The way our culture is organized is based on systemic inequality. The system itself has placed certain groups of people at a disadvantage. Structural inequality operates by norms, practices, attitudinal trends, and attitudes that build obstacles to achieving true equality or equal opportunity. We also see structural discrimination as structural bias, processes that continuously err in favor of one group and discriminate against others. There are situations where the underlying prejudice is not embedded in the belief of an individual concerning a person or group of persons, but in structural systems, be they civil or bureaucratic.

The existence of structural discrimination leaves the states with the challenge of adopting policies that look at the legal framework and other incentives, considering behavior patterns and how different institutions function. Human rights education may solve this question.

Forms of Intolerance and Discrimination

Xenophobia

Xenophobia, or fear of strangers, is a broad term that can be applied to any fear of someone other than yourself. Xenophobia is an unreasonable and unfounded fear of immigrants or outsiders because it is not inherently focused on any clear, objective danger posed by the so-called outsiders.

Xenophobia, as prejudice, relates to the false notion that it threatens people from other countries, groups, cultures, or languages. Xenophobia also becomes prejudice when there are manifestations of bigotry, including sexism and homophobia, but significant differences remain. Sexism, racism, and other types of discrimination are based on individual traits, and xenophobia is typically given to the belief that members of another group are foreign to the "natives' class."

Although xenophobia can be articulated in different ways, common characteristics include:

- Feeling awkward with people who have been classified as another "community."
- Going to great lengths to avoid specific locations
- Unwillingness to be friends with people solely because of their skin tone, dress style, or other specific factors
- Having trouble taking a boss seriously or communicating with a co-worker who is not of the same ethnic, cultural, or religious community, or the same gender

While it can reflect a genuine fear, most xenophobic people have no real phobia. Alternatively, the term is most often used to describe those who discriminate against refugees and foreigners.

Those who display xenophobia claim their society or country is superior or wish to keep foreigners out of their group and can even take part in acts that hurt those seen as outsiders.

There are two main xenophobia types:

> • **Cultural xenophobia:** Rejecting artifacts, customs, or symbols identified with another group or nationality. These can include language, clothes, music, and other culture-related customs.

> • **Immigrant xenophobia:** this type involves rejecting individuals who are believed to be outsiders.

This may mean denying people of various faiths or nationalities their due privileges and can lead to discrimination, hatred, aggression, and even genocide.

There's a common need to belong to a group — and heavy affiliation with a specific group may also be useful. But it may also contribute to the mistrust of others considered not to belong. It is natural, and even automatic, to protect a group's interests by removing threats to those interests. Unfortunately, this inherent defensive character also leads members of a party to shun or even threaten others considered unique, even though they do not pose any direct threat at all.

A Deeper Look into Racism

The expression 'racism' is often misunderstood. The Oxford Dictionary defines it as "Prejudice, discrimination, or antagonism directed against someone of another race based on the belief that one's race is superior." This definition, however, is nothing but a simplified explanation of a complicated issue.

Defining Race

The concept of a 'racial group' stems from certain long disproved anthropological theories. Mostly developed in Western Europe in the late nineteenth and early twentieth centuries, these theories, rooted in the assumption of white supremacy, assumed that human beings could be classified into racial groups based on physical and

87

behavioral traits linked to ethnicity, nationality, and related concepts such as common language.

Today, the everyday use of the words 'race' and 'ethnic' has increased. However, these false perceptions of ethnic distinction have been ingrained in society's attitudes and behaviors, especially in Western nations.

Perils of Racism

Of all the evil and violent psychological and social disorders that can infect human beings and have affected the world's peoples' history and lives, rival racisms and its destructive effect, are evil whether raw and unmasked or camouflaged and hidden. It is an assault upon humanity and an awful insult to divinity. To grasp and comprehend racism's aggressive and damaging nature, we have to differentiate it from the racial discrimination with which it is frequently associated.

Racial discrimination is hatred and animosity against a human being focused on biological distinctions perceived as indicators of defectiveness. Racism is the incorporation of the hate and hostility into public policy and socially accepted practice.

Never accepting someone once they seem to be genetically distinctive is racial discrimination and unreasonable. Exploiting those distinctions to control, manipulate, abuse, murder, validate, and create this brutality as a legal and social tradition is racism. One may dislike or be hostile to others who look visually different.

Still, racism is ingrained in the social structure itself, woven into legislation and public policy, and accepted by society, both publicly and implicitly, actively and unconsciously.

Racism expresses itself in three primary ways:

1) Imposition;
2) Ideology; and
3) Institutional arrangements.

Discrimination begins as *an imposition*, an act of massive violence, and continues in various forms. This becomes its defining feature, distinguishing it from mere prejudice. Violence equates to acts of dominance that involve multiple kinds of destruction from invasion, conquest, and occupation to enslavement and dispossession, ethnic cleansing, genocide, and the holocaust. This is followed by acts of continued violence to maintain race control and dominance, including African Americans, after extended enslavement, massacres, lynching, police violence, and other forms of systemic violence, including deprivation of the necessities of life.

The Implications of Intolerance (In our Everyday Living Routine)

Tolerance is not merely an abstract virtue; it considerably affects the public affairs of society. Man is a social being and must work with others in a spirit of peace and collaboration. A fair amount of willingness to give-and-take is needed in this process, a capacity for compromise.

MICHAEL CARTER

We cannot persuade other people until we will be equally influenced by exercising a good nature.

Intolerance separates human beings, establishing a feeling of eternal isolation between them. Due to the absence of a moral sense of tolerance, disputes, uprisings, hatred, pride, discrimination, dehumanization, repression, and violence dominate our political system, religious affairs, and communities.

There are political controversies everywhere. Several nations that do not wish other countries to make improvements are always imposing sanctions on them. Politicians don't accept each other. They are all seeking to downplay their rivals' strong administration.

Even when we take a cursory look at our social affairs, we are aware of the repression and persecution of religious minorities. The faiths are split into various denominations. Over the centuries, this has caused the bloodshed of countless innocent people.

The Way Out of Intolerance

The problem of intolerance can only be tackled if we are all involved.

What Can Individuals Do?

1. People should actively center their daily lives on being accommodating of others. It includes

actively questioning the assumptions usually found when testing others.

2. Follow the *Golden Rule*, "Treat others the same as you would want them to treat you."

3. Begin seeing differences as a good thing. It will also be helpful to learn about cultural distinctions. Instead of being afraid and dismissive of other people, you can think about their differences and appreciate them.

4. Don't blame an entire racial community, ethnicity, etc. for the evil acts of a minority who belong to the same class.

5. Remember that we all share the same world. No matter what our differences are, we all belong to this universe. To be tolerant is to accept and even rejoice in those distinctions.

What Can the Press Do?

Practically, the press has a vital role to play in suppressing intolerance. This can be done by intentionally killing opinionated instigating news, refusing to advertise views that encourage discrimination, and using positive images to promote understanding and cultural sensitivity.

What Can the Educational System Do?

The root cause of intolerance is a lack of awareness, comprehension, and a propensity to view the world in black and white with no gray areas. Hence, fighting prejudice has to be included in education at all levels. Often, intolerance is associated with an inflated sense of self-righteousness and ego. It is perpetuated by systems that are political, national, or religious. Such ideas are learned from an early age and absorbed. Therefore, greater emphasis needs to be placed on encouraging higher education institutions to educate the young mind about the basics of morality. There is needs to be more effort to teach children about diversity and civil rights. Children and young people should be encouraged to be open-minded and curious at home, in schools, and everywhere.

Schools and other educational establishments should include inclusion in their curriculum to educate the young mind. Inclusion doesn't have to mean that you agree with another's way of life, beliefs, and practices; it means you refrain from discriminating against them because they are different. However, it should be remembered that education is a lifetime journey that does not start or finish at school or university. Tolerance building by schooling cannot be significant until it meets all ages and happens everywhere: at home (with the parents), in classrooms, and at work.

International Bodies

International organizations continue to adopt the values of democratic equality. The United Nations, for example, has also established The Declaration of Moral Principles on Tolerance, accepted and signed in Paris on November 16, 1995, by the 185-member states of UNESCO, which recognizes tolerance as a social, political, and legal necessity for persons, groups, and governments. I also know that the Red Cross preaches tolerance. I propose that the principle of tolerance be accepted and distributed as widely as possible through other foreign bodies: EU, AU, UN, etc.

Governments

Governments should likewise aim to institutionalize tolerance policies. Long ago, international human rights law established that "Governments have three degrees of responsibility: honoring, preserving, and upholding any right."

- Respecting a right means not interfering with the enjoyment of the right.
- Protecting the right requires enacting laws to provide mechanisms for preventing State or non-state actors from violating the right. This defense is to be freely given to everyone.

- To achieve the right means to take active steps to establish institutions and procedures, including allocating resources, to enable people to enjoy the right.

From this understanding, I draw the expectation that racism, racial discrimination, xenophobia, and all other related forms of intolerance should be prohibited in the political and electoral sphere through active government policy and legislation.

There is no doubt about it, and tolerance is an essential attribute in our everyday lives. When we practice patience, we will be free from the pain of jealousy.

Sometimes there can be no tolerance, however. We should never tolerate moral corruption, social mistakes, political and financial dishonesty; we should never be complacent about attacks on our national integrity and our fundamental rights to the forces of progress within society.

CHAPTER 10
I SEE PEOPLE

"The outer world is a reflection of the inner world. Other people's perception of you is a reflection of them; your response to them is an awareness of you." - **Roy T. Bennett**

People are people everywhere you go. How you see them often has more to do with you than them. You have an absolute reality in your mind about people known as your perception, and this perception always affects the way you respond to these people. The truth of the matter is that while some of these perceptions of certain types of people have been subconsciously planted into your mind, for your location, the surrounding people, or certain situations you may have found yourself in, have become your reality. Even though you try, you cannot shake them off.

You need to understand, "The mistakes of one should not be the burden of all," and whether you like it, this is a learned perception, one which you must take time to flush out of your system.

You need to see people and not perceptions because people make up your reality, while perceptions are only concepts in your mind, in which the incorrect one you need to flush out.

Why do you have negative perceptions of other people?

As said earlier, the manner you see people are, for sure, factors that have caused you to have a general concept of others. It's just like "having one rotten apple and then condemning the entire tree." You end up losing the opportunity to get some of the best apples out there because you have a general misconception of just one tree. So why do you have negative perceptions of other people?

1. **Because we have been in a situation where other people from that geographical location have done something bad.** Think of this, the people from Iraq have a terrible rap with much of the world, mostly people from the United States, because of the actions of Osama Bin Laden, and this is a continuing trend as these countries do not want to interact with each other. Unfortunately, this mentality will cause those who are not even born yet to

have these perceptions because of their environment

2. **General Misconceptions of Certain People.** A general misconception of people is like a broad understanding of who people are and what they stand for. This is like a label we place on them, and most of the time, it affects even the best of individuals. We never choose where we are born; if we did, there would be places in the world that would have a scarce population and when you find yourself in a place where the people there seem to be perceived as good people, you take it as a right to judge rather than a privilege, and this is not the right way to go about things. Imagine how you would feel if the tables were turned; you would understand what it means to be labeled a certain way.

3. **Personal Experience.** Nothing hurts more than a proverbial knife in the back, especially from someone you care about. For some, this experience shapes their reality, which affects everyone else they come into contact with. I have seen a countless number of people ignore certain people just because of their name. Why is this the case? Because of the personal experience, they have had with a single person.

MICHAEL CARTER

You understand that even as you go through the pages of
this book, someone from your location, your hometown,
someone with the same name as you, could very well be
causing someone else to have a wrong perception of you,
and if we all have a terrible perception of one another, then
what is left but hate, war, and suffering?

The Diversity in Humanity

Humanity is a diverse race with many different tribes and
tongues and countless people, making the world a
wonderful place to live. I want you to imagine that
everyone in the world was the same as you. The first thing
that would come to mind is that the world would be a
better place.

This doesn't seem right because the world would not be
better; instead, it would become more boring and
predictable than ever, and this is not the right way to live
– even our maker knows this. For example, if one person
or even a group of people from a specific region did
something that annoyed you, you would have to
understand that life is often this way. The sooner you
realize that the better off you would be.

One thing I realize is that no one thrives under tense
conditions, no matter how good or bad they are, and when
you have a perception of someone because of a situation
you have encountered, it affects not only them; it affects
you. This is something you must recognize and deal with.

I SEE YOU

When you hold firm to negative perceptions, you put yourself in the wrong spot. You live with your defense up, ready, and waiting for someone to make a wrong move or mistreat you somehow. Give yourself a break. The sooner you realize that this is as bad for you as it is for that person on your "negative" hit list, the better for you.

The Way You See Others is a Projection of Who You Are

Sometimes we cannot appreciate the differences that make us so unique, and we sometimes want everyone to be exactly like us. The love we have for others is defined by what we see in ourselves, and as for those things are not in us, we despise them.

The way people behave is a big test of our awareness. Sometimes, when people have difficulty breaking habits, especially ones that we don't understand, we get irritated as we see no reason this should be. Now, this does not qualify you as a lousy person; one thing philosophy of humanity has taught us is that "*When your friends fail, you feel bad, but when that same friend tops you, you feel worse.*"

Even when this is the case, there is another side to the puzzle, and it is the fact that the way you perceive others influences the way you treat them if you see yourself, but it is also a mirror image of how others see themselves.

This might sound difficult, but we will break it down as we move on. People often have negative perceptions about themselves, mainly because they know the general

99

concept people have. This causes them to behave in specific ways, some of which we perceive as strange.

When they find themselves in the company of people who hold negative perceptions about them, their character aligns with that perception and idea. You would notice that no matter how "normal" some people seem, certain things find a way of happening to them, which is why people have a general perception of them. Negative self-worth slowly causes them to conform to what is said of them.

This happens because when we imagine that people have a particular thought about us, it affects how we react. We unknowingly conform to that image leading to more significant reactions, something which potentially harms us.

For example, if a man from Iraq or Afghanistan comes to America, and they look the part and dress the part, they may act more carefully than they would at home, making them appear even more suspicious than they would.

Maybe this person is trying his best to avoid rapid movements, but people suspect his slow progress. He feels people would think something is wrong if he keeps his hands in his pockets, so he keeps them out in the open as he walks, and people wonder what he has stashed in his pockets. He wants to do something as simple as going to the bathroom, but when people see him there, they feel he wants to plant something there, so they run. So, he stays where he is and tries to manage the situation, but he looks tense. People see him as anxious and assume something is about to happen. This results in a no-win case either for the foreigner or for those observing him.

A person's character can be born out of the idea that they are not good, but it came from the idea that people do not think they are good enough.

Have you ever felt this way? Felt an absolute disdain for someone or a group of people? Maybe you cannot point to the exact reason, and it might result from programmed misconceptions you have about them. You would most likely find that your mind meditates on thoughts that conform to those misconceptions. You paint this person or those in that light, even though what you perceive is not necessarily the case. Let me tell you, the more you continue on the path of incorrect preexisting judgments, the more you find those you judge conforming to the way you perceive them. As this continues, it gets to a certain point where these perceptions become a reality, and everything is affected.

I want you to understand this:

- Many people, both women, and men have a powerful attraction to confident people. And because of their high level of confidence, every other aspect of their lives, including some of their bad characteristics, are tolerated.

- Most of the so-called superstars you know today are unique and "Out of this World," Because they believe in themselves, people also see this confidence in them. Others who do not have the slightest clue about who they envy them because they perceive this confidence.

- Finally, you set the standard for how people would treat you with the way you treat yourself. In fact, "you are the one who would teach people how they should treat you" because people understand what is and what is not allowed. When you conform to everything around you, it is a sign of a lack of self-love, and others see this.

Realize that the picture you have of yourself influences how the world sees you. Therefore, if you feel negativity around people who are always negative, you may see yourself as a negative person. It will take some alone time to get a proper perspective of yourself.

Over time, people's perceptions will often snowball until we have no control over what we have started. I have a negative perception of you, and I show it. You see this perception and are affected by it, and it changes you. You ever so slightly conform to my perception. You offer a particular character type, and my conviction of who you are is falsely justified. I pass it on to the next generation, and they allow it to become part of who they are.

To make matters worse, you see no reason you should not conform; you are being hated for it already. This cultivates more hate over the years, and suddenly if someone were to ask us why we fight, we have no clue.

We should try to *see* people rather than rely on our perceptions of them. Many of the perceptions we have were planted into our subconscious by someone who had their perceptions. The line between reality and negative perceptions, and confirmation to those negative perceptions, is not as thin as you might have thought it to be.

I *See* People, and You Should Too, so the World can become a Better Place.

CHAPTER 11

I SEE CHANGE

"Never doubt that a small group of thoughtful, committed citizens can change the world. Indeed, it is the only thing that ever has." — **Margaret Mead**

Change is an essential rule of creation, transforming the old world into a new one for better development. According to Carlyle, "Stagnation is death." Even as an individual, if you are not changing, you are dying without knowing.

Change is always painful, but it is inevitable. "The history of the unchangeable is a figment of the fancy, an abstraction of the intellect unsupported by fact." That is the great lesson from which we learn that man dislikes change and likes to cling to the old order.
Humans are always reluctant to make changes or step out of their comfort zone. Change brings anxiety; perhaps

because people find safety and comfort is the thought of stability. In truth, change, though unavoidable, doesn't come so quickly.

Change is always greeted with opposition from whatever is incumbent. This is most likely because of an anxious, unfounded fear of the unknown.

Some traditions are reasonable and even necessary. Others, though, become a hindrance to a better future because they cloud what could be. Like flowing water is wholesome, and stagnant water is toxic, so are customs and traditions which can only refresh and attractive if it regularly transforms with change.

Unless the people of our nation and the world embrace change, our society will stay static. Author and pastor Rick Warren once said, "There is no growth without change, no change without fear or loss and no loss without pain." If we look at our world around us, it was created for change. If there were no change, we wouldn't have butterflies, seasons, better consumer products, etc. Therefore, we must brace ourselves for growth to remain in sync with the ever-changing material world. If transformation is rejected, it can lead to societal disintegration and deterioration. This is because the societal breakdown is the natural consequence of an inability to change in tandem with time.

Think about the change in your own life. How are you different from you were five years ago? Ten years ago? What about the people around you like your family and your friend group? Your thoughts, and sometimes even your values evolve. How you perceive change affects your ability to embrace it.

Accept Changes

Change can be a positive development, but too frequently, it faces opposition. This aversion emanates from concern or fear of the unforeseen consequences that this change may bring. While we cannot regulate or even foresee what changes will be presented daily, the change will happen! As Heraclitus once said, "The only constant in life changes."

Shifting our thinking to one that embraces change as a positive necessity in our lives and careers usually encourages us to excel. Change is inevitable and represents progress as we advance in a manner that produces greater efficiency and/or effectiveness.

The change will happen whether or not we like it. Tomorrow is going to differ from today. We might resist it, but it's somewhat like standing in a river and trying to keep the water back – futile. We can ignore, observe, embrace, or take part in the change actively unfolding around us.

However, our goal should be to embrace change and understand that we have a role to play in bringing it about. Leadership sets the tone, and everyone contributes. Yes, it can be stressful and daunting, but change also helps us grow and venture into new, unfamiliar territory, which will open doors we didn't even know existed.

For instance, it took me a long time to get used to a touchscreen when I first went from a Blackberry to a Smartphone. I was used to typing on a physical keyboard even though it was way too small for my fingers! I now have several touchscreen devices and use various applications to make my work more productive, innovative, and competitive.

We live in a global and multi-cultural economy, and we do business with people around the world. Most organizations around the world today have employees, clients, customers, vendors, and other stakeholders who communicate and collaborate daily to achieve desired results. Every day we face changes in our economy, markets, industries, organizations, technologies, and a change in leadership and people within our businesses. When we can get comfortable with this and wake up to embrace and welcome change every day, we are opening ourselves up to endless opportunities and possibilities.
Managing change is an essential skill in leadership today. Change not only requires leaders and managers to embrace it, but we all play a critical role, as individuals, in the execution of significant change.

Change is a positive thing; it's inevitable, essential and leads to improvement more often than not.

Ben Franklin said, "Life is ten percent what you make it and ninety percent how you take it." Embracing that concept requires one to step out of his comfort zone. However, doing so leads to beautiful results as we develop our awareness and our experiences.

One motto I've embraced is, "Get comfortable being uncomfortable." If we do, we are genuinely changing and opening up a world of possibility that we would not know otherwise as people grow and evolve when we are flexible and actively searching for and experimenting with new habits, approaches, talents, and information in ways that stretch us. Would you make it a priority? Welcome change and embrace it as a requirement for growth?

When we accept change as a positive necessity, we will not see it as an obstacle but an opportunity.

There are lots of proven practices and models for how leaders and managers can manage change. What can each person do to implement and execute change? I've learned to handle change effectively with ACT and have taught individuals and teams to do so.

ACT Now to Address Change Effectively

> ➤ Accept and recognize the need for change.
> ➤ Communicate proactively with all parties involved to clarify and understand the needs and processes required to implement the change.
> ➤ Thrive through the transformation that brings development — Throw yourself into change, have an open mind, try new ideas, explore alternative strategies, care about its effect on others, ask for

input and be available to everyone, showing them what you are also learning.

Change and Personal Growth

The notion of change can be upsetting. Many of us would like to stay away from change, whether it's large or small. The difference is an integral part of the personal path of growth, and we should welcome most of it. Change influences all facets of life but accepting change in your life will make an immense difference in healthy personal growth.

The Internal Change Will Help You

Change allows you to become the person you wish to be. One of the most satisfying tasks that you'll ever experience is to embrace and enact change yourself. This also shows an important life skill. When you're able to recognize areas in your life that you are dissatisfied with, or areas that require growth in your personal and professional life, you are on the road to success.

Generally, it is necessary to regularly make internal changes to prevent becoming stagnant even if it's changing the way you present yourself, improving your expertise, attending a workshop, or adjusting your daily routine.

The External Change Will Shape You

There are individual transitions that we can't control. Circumstances and changes will often dramatically affect our lives. Change you can't prevent, however positive or negative it sounds at the moment, can teach you something vital to your growth. External change makes you more open, more aware, and prepares you for the future. As much as the internal change will motivate you to go forward, the external change will give you the confidence to push ahead.

Change Gives Hope

Whether it's prompted by you or organically started, change is your way out of any circumstance or position you're frustrated or disappointed within your life and environment. As soon as you accept change, you're going to realize that your current condition doesn't have to last forever, and it enables you to step into something bigger and better. When you ignore change, you lose the ability to develop and grow. It is time to view change as something positive in your life with positive outcomes.

Change Makes You Happier

You're going to be happier. Personal development and intentional positive transformation are related to happiness as they connect with heart issues. For every movement toward your well-being, you experience inward joy. The deliberate change also helps you deal with stressors and challenges constructively, which decreases discomfort and promotes personal mental well-being. Accepting yourself and trying to be the healthiest version of you through gradual change creates a mysterious harmony and brings you into a greater happiness level.

I SEE YOU

Change Helps You to Move On

Memories can hold you back if you allow them to. Your bitter experiences of past days can threaten your tomorrow if you are not careful. It takes those little daily changes to pull you from the quicksand of bad memories.

Therefore, no matter what has happened in your past, you need to stick to your development plan. As you continue on the path of personal growth, it forces you to change, which helps you leave the past and step into the future, you've always dreamed of obtaining.

Progress Means Change

When you believe that your progress is sluggish and you are miles away from your professional and personal ambitions, look back at how far you've come. You likely have made improvements over the past year alone, even if the changes are small. If you look back at the past four years, you will see a lot more progress than you expected. If you are not impressed by the path ahead of you, making a change could increase your financial worth, live a healthier lifestyle, or even affect a sense of fulfilment. Your target should be to continually make improvements and make changes that will ultimately be profitable.

Anyway, Change Will Happen

Change is an essential part of personal growth and cannot occur without the other. You may see yourself as someone who doesn't want change, but it's crucial to note that change is unavoidable. Change doesn't come to you and ask for your permission. It's going to happen with or without your consent. There are specific changes you could take control of in your decisions and your life. So, it is better to accept and embrace change and do your best to make it your own along the way.

Social Change

Social change is a term that many of us take for granted or cannot grasp. No culture has ever remained the same – EVER! Growth continues to happen. They embrace transition, see it as necessary. Sociologists describe social change as changes that affect cultural and social processes in human experiences and relationships. Such changes take place over time, which can have significant long-term social implications; well-known examples of this change range from social campaigns in civil rights, women's rights, LBGT rights, and more. Relationships have changed, institutions have changed, and societal expectations have changed because of these social reform campaigns. What concerns me, and what I think everyone should be involved with, is our mutual ability to affect societal progress and effect change. Although we recognize that change is inevitable, we don't have to believe that we are helpless in its path. It is the degree to which we think about the course of social progress that we will seek and influence it and help build the sort of "change we want to see in the world."

I SEE YOU

Change Starts with You

Most of us waste a lot of time waiting for other people in our lives to change. For many years I thought the same way. I spent years of my childhood, waiting on family and friends to change. I invested much of my adult working life wanting clients and my coworkers to change.

Sometimes we even believe we should change them. We do so in the pretext of "helping" them become better individuals, but what's going on is that we're trying to transform them in ways that fit ourselves, satisfy our desires, and keep ourselves happier.

As I journey through life, one thing I've learned is that we can't change others. It will not work. It's a waste of time, effort, and resources.

I have seen wives who try to change their husbands, guys trying to change their girlfriends, young adolescents attempting to change their family members, and parents overly frustrated trying to change their adult children. You cannot change others; however, you can change yourself.

Many people believe that somehow the other person keeps them from being happy with their lives.

Happiness is inner work. Gandhi, while holding many religious beliefs than my own, was the one who taught me this fundamental lesson. He realized that his effort couldn't change other people. Ironically, Gandhi is also a man credited with creating more people's change in his day. How could he?

The answer came from Gandhi, **"You must be the change you wish to see in others."**

People react mostly to what we do, not to what we profess. Leader and motivator John Maxwell said, "People don't care how much you know until they know how much you care." It is called learned behavior. Children, for example, will generally align and mimic the attitudes and actions they continuously observe.

In doing and becoming what you wish them to be, you encourage them to feel motivated to improve. The result is that change becomes long term, as the impetus for improvement originated from the other person, not from you.

Trying to get other people to change by believing that you can change them doesn't work. Instead of focusing on bringing others to change, try encouraging others by attempting to improve yourself.

When we change ourselves, our perceptions about our situations, the people involved change too. That is how we "get" other people to change.

CHAPTER 12
I SEE UNITY

"The reason why the world lacks unity and lies broken and in heaps is because man is disunited with himself." — **Ralph Waldo Emerson**

Most of us have heard of the phrase, "United we stand divided we fall." It is a hundred percent correct.

The great and wise King Solomon said in Ecclesiastes 4:12, "Though another may overpower one, two can withstand him. And a threefold cord is not quickly broken." I rephrase it this way, "Unity grants us bravery and power."

It is easier to achieve your goals in a typical workplace when working together as a team and not as individuals.

MICHAEL CARTER

As John Maxell said, "Teamwork indeed makes the dreamwork!

These days support groups are ubiquitous, providing people opportunities to help and encourage one another. It's clear that when you operate as a team, the likelihood of success drastically increases.

For any business to expand, for example, there must be a coming together of willing hands and smart heads. It speeds growth up by unity of strength.

We humans should always stand together because unity not only gives strength but also is essential for survival. It is significant to note that even among animals, an agreement is necessary for success and survival. For instance, when any dolphin gets injured, other dolphins help that wounded dolphin by taking her out of the water to breathe and live. Soldier ants don't move alone. They move in millions. That's why they can't easily be destroyed. Colonies can have over 15 million workers and can transport 3000 preys per hour. That's amazing!

I'm sure you also know that locusts move in swarms. The swarms are enormous masses of locusts. There could be 50 million locusts packed in half a square mile space. That's why they climb obstacles quickly, quench fires along their journey and survive season after season.

When you are part of a team, to be successful, you permit no outside force to influence you and break your unity negatively.

116

I SEE YOU

I'm reminded of a story in which a father called over his four sons and gave them each a stick and told them to break it. All four sons quickly broke their sticks. He then asked them to break 100 sticks that were tied together. The group of sticks could not be split! Teaching them a vital life lesson, the man said, "When you fight one another and stay alone, anyone can defeat you. But when you stay together, just as the lump of sticks could not be broken, no one will break and trounce you."

Importance of Unity

1. We need unity for survival.

History teaches us the significance of oneness. Nothing can rock or unsettle a nation if we unite it. Disunity in war is a recipe for disaster. During the American Civil War, former President Abraham Lincoln said, "A divided house cannot survive."

Unity is necessary for survival in all life situations. If one is self-centered, thinking of individual success and achievement instead of the team's overall interest, that may be detrimental to the team. From medieval history to call centers for Business Process Outsourcing, the team's concept has been a critical ingredient for success. How valid is the acronym, *TEAM,* which stands for, "**T**ogether, **E**veryone **A**chieves **M**ore?"

Families are another example of *TEAM.* Even when families disagree, argue, and bicker among themselves, often they resolve their differences, if for nothing more than to give the outside world a united facade. In families

117

with no tidying up of crises and rifts, greedy relatives can exploit the family.

2. Unity Protects.

A ten-year-old can kill a snake wandering around by itself. All that is needed is a little courage and one good strike. But who can tackle 15 snakes moving together? You don't need a prophet to tell you it's safe to attack a group of snakes.

3. Unity gives courage.

Whenever you see injustice and feel you should say something, it may be challenging to think alone. But once you get the support of other people, you become courageous and can easily stand up against that injustice.

4. Unity provides freedom.

Unity gives us liberty and helps us to succeed. Most of us can work or even possess the capacity to run our own business, but we can only maximize our success if we work together. Individually we're like a single drop of water, but together we're like an ocean. As you journey through life, you will meet many people with various backgrounds, and many of them will know something that you don't know. Think of how profitable it would be to combine your knowledge with theirs to pursue a common goal. What you struggle to accomplish alone becomes much easier when you work with another person and labor together in unity

I SEE YOU

Causes of Disunity

Disunity is a lack of agreement between people, and it keeps them from working together successfully. Disunity decreases efficiency. This is not only true in family, business, and war; it is right.

- For a seed to turn into a flowering plant, it requires the unity of soil, light, and water. The absence of one of these factors may be detrimental to the seed.

- A vehicle needs the cooperation of engine components to start and move. The lack of one part hinders the vehicle from operating as it should.

- A human needs food, clothing, and shelter to stay alive. Life can be shortened or, at the least, severely impaired if one of the three is lacking.

- To win any war, all the soldiers involved must work together in cooperation!

The importance of unity, therefore, cannot be overemphasized.

Here are some causes of disunity that must be eliminated in us.

1. "They're Different from Us," Mindset.

"They're Different from Us" is an assessment by people who feel that their way of life or power is threatened. By attempting to manipulate the common understanding of

119

what's going on, what's right, and what's likely, this social argument uses bias to encourage distrust and discord within and across cultures.

Today's autocrats recognize that when inequalities of ethnicity, gender, and religion are highlighted and exploited, empathy for the oppressed and mistreated is jeopardized. This is why so many apologists for the "They're Different from Us" mindset highlight these disparities while underplaying similarities in the fears and ambitions that we all share. If this tactic works, it divides groups that might otherwise form a more powerful, effective, and united resistance. When such coalitions fail to materialize, the defenders of massive inequality prevail, and the common good suffers.

What makes these arguments that "they differ from us" socially successful is that we consider members of the "elite group" more positively than members of the peasantry. Usually, when we are persuaded that someone belongs to the same group that we do, we see them as trustworthy and reliable, we hold them in high esteem, and we are more likely to share resources. This optimistic attitude reflects our perception that we have a lot in common with those people. Even if we have never met them, we can believe that their values, attitudes, and experiences in life are probably similar to ours. But if we see people as members of a distinct group, we likely won't care about their welfare as much, and there's a greater chance that we will see them as adversaries rather than partners. This is one of the principal reasons for social disunity.

2. Religious Intolerance.

Strife and disunity over religion have been here for thousands of years and remain unresolved. In reality, religious-based conflict is on the rise all over the world. In the US, the most recent FBI statistics show that religious faith is the second most targeted social category of hate crimes for the third year in a row. Hate crimes focused on religion account for twenty-two percent of bias-motivated offenses, the highest proportion ever in FBI monitoring history. Religious hate crimes in the US disproportionately target minority religions, especially Jews and Muslims, and report attacks on Catholics, Protestants, and other Christians.

Adherents of every faith prefer to assume that their religion is the sole source of the absolute truth. The way it presents is exclusive and definitive, and that the strategies it adopts to achieve salvation are unique and better than the others. This assertion to superiority and ultimacy creates an environment of conflict between followers of different religions and results in violence and hatred between them. Rather than trying to convince those who believe differently by sharing the tenants of the faith, and subsequently living in a way that represents their religion, many people look down on those people, showing how they treat them.

Various societies adopt tolerance of others and, in particular, religions to avoid open conflict. The first-ever use of the word 'tolerance' is dated back to the 15th century. It is defined in the *Oxford English Dictionary* as

"The activity or practice of suffering or experiencing pain or hardship; the strength or ability to withstand."

In the 16th century, after Queen Elizabeth I allowed the Puritans to carry out their activities with which she did not share or give consent, tolerance gained a new political meaning, "The acts of allowing, approving, allowing by law." It was permission granted by the sovereign state to break from the standard.

One consequence of the above use is that tolerance is the right of those with relative power over others.

Therefore, tolerance is a realization of those with power that people choose to live their lives the way they see fit. It follows then that intolerance is an attitude that allows us to show feelings of opposition and disapproval and taking adverse action to make others conform to a perceived standard of living.

3. Racial Discrimination or Racism.

Racism assumes that all race members possess unique characteristics or abilities, particularly in defining it as being superior or inferior to another race or races. Because of this, racism has once again become a huge topic over the last few years. Racism is hazardous in several ways and can tear apart any society.

No matter what shape or form it presents itself, racial prejudice is harmful. It is seen in many places from the train to the neighborhood, from the supermarket to the hospital, from the roadside to the crime scene. Statistics reveal that 38% of young people (13-17 years) have perceived racism online, while 43% of them reported that they observed it in school (pewsocialtrends.org, *On Views on Race and Racism, Blacks and Whites Are Miles Apart*).

Experiencing racism makes you feel insecure. Meanwhile, no one wants to find themselves in a place where they feel vulnerable. If one party discriminates unfairly against another, this could mean that these groups will not want to be around each other. There is no community. When people don't come together, obviously there will be no community. And once there is no community, there can be no unity.

Overcoming Disunity and Racism

Racism comes from a place of ignorance. Racists are not deep thinkers. Real thinkers know how stupid it is to exhibit racism. Not that all racists are inherently stupid, but we can say they are mostly ignorant.

A new Dartmouth College study presents some interesting ideas on racial prejudice and the brain. Racism can cause stupidity, according to the widely publicized results of this research. Even professors from highly regarded universities like Stanford are quoted as saying things like, "Racism makes people dumb."

Well, that makes a satisfying sound bite, but it is not a hundred percent accurate.

Here are what happened. White study participants who displayed racism toward Black people performed poorly after being tested by an African American individual on a cognitive skills test. The more prejudiced the subjects were (based on their scores from the Harvard implicit association test), the worse they performed.

What is interesting about this research is that it is the first to show, by magnetic resonance imaging, that there is a particular region of the brain correlated with attempts to say or do the correct thing. This portion of the brain having "executive control" has shown increased activity during the implicit association test and the interview. Those who received ratings showing a more definite disadvantage in this field had the most movement in their minds. They tried to keep themselves from making racial decisions or derogatory statements. Because this small little brain segment became overwhelmed, participants were momentarily unable to conduct thought-provoking activities.

So, the exact concept here really isn't just that racism makes you look stupid. It's that someone we have a racist contempt for inhibits our ability to think. If you live in a reasonably homogeneous culture, then the bias and part of your brain's "executive control" is not checked. However, once you interact with people, you have racial discrimination against daily, and your thinking gets compromised, at least temporarily.

What does this imply in the long term? Are racist people "dumbed down" in integrated communities because their over-imposed brains cannot cope with the presence of their "adversaries?" Is the impact cumulative? There needs to be a whole lot more research in these areas.

I SEE YOU

No rational person wants to admit that they may have a racial bias. We know that having a negative view of anyone based on race is disrespectful, unfounded, and damaging. We also know that this is politically incorrect and socially unacceptable. We like to believe that we are wise enough to ignore some subtle forms of racism that lurk our minds.

Well, our brains don't know this. These tests test what happens in our minds, not what we want to see happening. The results could be surprising.

The good news is there is a section of our brain that is trying to act appropriately! This study was done at Dartmouth College, with informed, knowledgeable, reasonably progressive white students. Though they do not indicate it in the report, they probably did not even consider themselves racist. What occurs if we perform the same analysis among others who freely confess their prejudice?

If we understand better and want to stop being racist, how are we going to do that? The answer is to have a better understanding of each other and to attempt to establish constructive relationships. Having regular contact alone cannot eradicate racism.

Consider your brain and your inclination regarding race. The initial step is to be straightforward and honest: everyone on the planet has a racial predisposition or likeness. The next stage is to reflect and examine yourself to discover where you stand.

And afterward? What's next?

We learn racism. And with what we know about how the brain works: anything we learned previously can be unlearned!

Understand all that you can about different ethnicities and races. Peruse, travel, see movies, listen to music, try new foods - do everything conceivable to build up a genuine interest and authentic concern for individuals from other races.

Try building associations with people of distinct races and cultures. With enough knowledge and work, you can outmaneuver your own mind's prejudice, not by being color blind, but by being color appreciative.

CHAPTER 13

I SEE GENERATIONS

"Each generation imagines itself to be more intelligent than the one that went before it, and wiser than the one that comes after it." — **George Orwell**

One of the most mysterious revelations I received is that everything needed for the future is already available. It is available in a distinct form. For instance, in its seed form, the food consumed in a thousand years is present in this generation. After planted and germinated, the seed will produce fruit that will subsequently produce seeds that will then become food for the next generation. Likewise, people who in the future will either build or destroy nations, discover cures, or commit genocide are inside us now, even though we cannot see them yet.

This revelation made me realize that it connects every generation tangibly. More so even than I had ever

127

assumed. It would seem then that since future generations are inside of us, we are the future generations!

Therefore, if our current generation doesn't play the role it must, then the consequence will negatively affect the subsequent generation. Frantz Fanon said, "Every generation, out of relative obscurity, must discover its purpose, either to fulfill it or to betray it." Everyone has a role to play that will affect the future, and for the next generation to thrive, we must come together in unity.

You are the future, and the future is in you. What future generations will become lies in the seed already planted in you. No matter how old you are, you should act with this understanding.

Personally, this line of thought has forced me to think differently about how different generations affect each other. I see generations after me repeating many of the same mistakes that this current generation is making. Therefore, if we will help the next generation be better than the current generation, then our generation has to be better, especially as it relates to how we treat each other.
Today, we may decide to satisfy some current urge. However, realizing that those decisions directly affect future generations, it is important to weigh those decisions against the backdrop of future implications. Every single action you take has a direct effect on the future. Every move is a seed planted in your generation. Suppose you are sincere about intentionally making the world a better place. In that case, it is essential only to do things that will

produce beneficial fruit, not only to this generation but to those to come.

How People See Generations

Since the beginning of time, young people have always believed that they have a better perspective on life and how the world should work because it ties older people to outdated traditions and is unwilling to change. Likewise, more senior people believe that their perspective is the correct one because young people are inexperienced, spontaneous, and reluctant to listen to wisdom. The world is continuously changing, and every generation has something to offer.

The world has experienced more changes and advancements in technology in the last 30 years than perhaps all of its history. Think about the incredible development in communication; how in the late 1990s and early 2000s, we almost instantly pivoted from paper mail to instant electronic messages? In the last decade, because of cellular technology, phone booths have become extinct. In the entertainment industry, the quality of digital displays and digital sound has increased exponentially.

When you consider these types of technological advances and the strides made in other industries, it is easy to see why the current generation feels better than the former. But does this sped up development alone really make this generation better than any other age? Some may argue that more significant technological advances have led to a less relational society and a greater dependence on technology, thus a diminishing mental capacity for critical thinking.

If we are going to compare generations, maybe we should look at other differences. For example, the older generation may concede that technology we have in place they would've never dreamed of but feel that when it comes to morality and character, our society is at an all-time low. Perceived transgressions that were taboo are now being perpetrated without the slightest modicum of guilt.

Older people may argue that some older generation advantages include lower criminal activity, a stronger work ethic, greater political participation, and a greater desire to participate in voluntary organizations. All of this is debatable based on perception.

Just as our perceptions of each other based on politics, color, culture, and gender harm us, our perceptions of each other based on the generation to which we belong divides us even more. While it's true that we are all created differently with our uniqueness, the overwhelming desire for independence and individuality can sometimes hinder the sense of community that brings fulfillment to a society.

In an article written by Jenée Mendillo of *Bayshore Home Care,* she says, "In the recent past, extended families often lived within the same home or very close to each other; however, this does not occur as frequently today. Even though people live healthier, longer lives, they expect to be self-sufficient. The trend in recent decades is for older

Americans to live alone. Because of this desire for independence, either by nuclear families or older adults, only one in eight single elderly adults now lives with extended family. The paradox is that although children today are more likely to have healthy, active grandparents, they are also less likely to know their grandparents well or visit with them frequently."

The Balance

One would then be pushed to ask rightly:

- Is the older generation better?
- Is the new better?
- Is one any better than the other?

The truth, though, is that living in different eras could cause people to have different perspectives on how life should be lived. The exposure one will determine how highly or lowly the person rates his or her generation. There is no *better* generation. The success and fulfillment of age depending on the effort the people give toward making their generation better.

I am convinced that generations can only get better if we all seek to unify our efforts in making it better. This is a deliberate process and includes developing a collective desire to establish justice and peace.

What then can we do to reap the benefits of intergenerational relationships?

1. **Avoid conclusions based on fallacies.** People often associate other peoples' ages with the way they live their life. They assume that because a particular set of people are old, they think in a specific way. Looking at how some young people address more senior people; one can tell just how shortsighted they are in judging the older generation.

To address a person with contempt and a lack of respect because of their age is also prejudice. This has, in part, contributed to loneliness in older people, and more people die from loneliness than actual illnesses. If we are to set the record straight, everyone must avoid judging people by their age.

Another popular fallacy is that the world keeps changing, and because of that, it is getting worse. The book of Ecclesiastes 1:9 (CEV) clarifies that "Everything that is happening has happened before; nothing is new, nothing under the sun!" We see vintage outfits gradually surface again and again in fashion, and the clothes we used to refer to as vintage or old schools have become new trends. Eventually, the current trends will become vintage again. As the world turns, and time marches on, no generation is better than another. In many respects, we keep renouncing a particular way of life, only to return to it again.

2. **Embrace change.** Irrespective of the moment you find yourself in, it is essential to embrace this time in your life. Rejecting all change is simply like fighting against yourself or beating the wind. Imagine what a person's life would be like if they left to change and remain in the past, despite introducing machines that make the industry more

efficient. Insisting on using telegraphs to send messages in an era where mobile phones have provided easier and faster access will ostracize you. We can find wisdom in Ecclesiastes 3:1 (CEV), "Everything on earth has its own time and its season." Do not constrain yourself to that which you used to be. Be renewed. Self-discipline should not stop you from accessing those things that would make life better for you.

3. Consider the Concept of Equity. There is a difference between equality and equity. We should all be equal when it comes to how we are *treated* and how we treat others. However, sometimes equity is better than equality. Equality is giving several people the same share. Assume that you are caring for three hungry children. Equality means that you would give them the same amount of food to eat. On the other hand, Equity, while still fair and impartial, implies that one would distribute portions according to the needs of the people. For example, if three hungry people came to you and had a loaf of bread, equality is giving each hungry person one-third of the loaf. Equity, however, is giving each person a portion according to his or her level of hunger. The greediest people will take the most significant share, while others will take what they need according to their desire. This prevents any bread from being wasted.

Practicing equity in everything you do has the advantage of ensuring that people genuinely get their needs met. Every generation has needs at different times, and those needs should be completed accordingly.

4. Close the Gap. Achieving better intergenerational relationships starts with you. Be that person who makes the difference by doing what you can to close the generation gap. The generation gap only causes a divide when we allow our perceptions to drive our actions toward others. Be that person who brings everyone together. We understand that there are significant benefits in an intergenerational relationship, not only for the people involved but for society.

In that same article written by Jenée Mendillo, she says that intergenerational relationships can:

1. Provide an opportunity for both to learn new skills.
2. Give the child and the older adult a sense of purpose.
3. Help to ease fears children may have of the elderly.
4. Help children to understand and later accept their aging.
5. Invigorate and energize older adults.
6. Help reduce the likelihood of depression in the elderly.
7. Reduce the isolation of older adults.
8. Fill a void for children who do not have grandparents available to them.
9. Help keep family stories and history alive.
10. Aide in cognitive stimulation and broaden social circles should a youth introduce technology into a senior's life.

I SEE YOU

Great things happen when we embrace unity and love. If we see ourselves, not only as of the hope for future generations but as the future generations themselves, then we would genuinely touch the lives of those who come after us. The future generation is already here; they are inside you and me now.

I see a future generation where relationships are done well. I know this generation is manifesting the full potential that God has purposed for it. To make this a reality, we must ourselves become conscious that we are this generation!

"Every generation, out of relative obscurity, must discover its own purpose, either to fulfill it or to betray it." - Frantz Fanon

The ball is now in your court.

CHAPTER 14
MY IDENTITY, MY WORLD VIEW

"It is always good to explore the stuff you don't agree with to understand a different lifestyle or foreign worldview. I like to be challenged in that way, and always end up learning something I didn't know." - **Laura Linney**

Your worldview is the way you identify with the world. The way you see things, your perception of how the world works. Your worldview is connected to your identity because it is the way you perceive things and, therefore, the way you expect things to go, sort of like a status quo you have in your mind about how the world ought to function.

You have this mindset, and when things do not go in that direction, often you have a problem with it, and in this problem lies a particular character you portray, and that reveals your identity. According to the quote by Laura Linney, she understands that exploring new things would help her see things from another perspective, shaping a personality different from the stiff and one-sided one you used to have. Before now, I had a specific comprehensive view that included people who did certain things. Somehow, I was shielded from situations that put me in a position to decide whether I would make the same decision.

At a certain point, my shield came down, and I found myself in a position where I had to decide whether or not to go in that direction. It was one of the hardest decisions for me to make, and even though I did not go in the order I eventually despised, I understood what made them choose that path and why nobody should judge them for their actions but look for a way to see things from their perspective carefully.

Even the Bible in Proverbs 4, Verse 23 states, "Guard your heart with all diligence for out of it are life issues." Without the right worldview, others' lack of conformity to your personal beliefs breeds contempt because you see it as the wrong way to live, and you react accordingly as it is in your heart.

If you grew up in a family who forced you to live a certain way, as you get older, you would always have it in the back of your mind to live exactly that way. When you find yourself in certain situations in life, this mindset would ever come to light, and you would respond accordingly.

According to an article from *Psychology Today*, "Identity may be gained indirectly from parents, peers, and other role models." Children come to define themselves in terms of how they think their parents see them. If their parents see them as worthless, they will come to identify themselves as ineffective. People who perceive themselves as likable may remember more positive than negative statements.

Factors that Influence Our World View

In this section of the book, we will take a close look at the factors that influence our worldview. It would give us a more unobstructed view of how our subconscious shapes us and how some of these things happen without understanding how the process takes hold of us.

Secondary Influences

If at an early stage in life, you had access to certain things like books that had positive influences on you and how you think, some negative factors you might come across along the way may not harm you. I am making the point here that our perception of self and how we perceive the world is a function of multiple influences (social, parental, and cultural). Though we may not realize it, these things help shape us, and it is only when we deliberately explore these factors that we can fully understand the layers that make us who we are and how we perceive the world.

I have mentioned this twice, and people think this is something we automatically know, but you might be surprised by what influences you and your perception of the world and how much we take it for granted.

I SEE YOU

Personal Experiences

Are you physically fit? If you are, then maybe you have no clue what people who have one disability feel. Are you prosperous, or at least financially stable? Most of the time, you cannot understand what it means not to have something to eat or have clothes to wear or even a roof over your head. Are you a man? You do not understand what it means to be a woman and how it has been a social norm in most cultures to treat women as a weaker, less intelligent gender.

Other things, such as being able to breathe fresh air, drink clean water, and have the freedom to worship as you wish, are things that we often take for granted. The truth is that we have no clue what it is like to be in another person's shoes who don't enjoy those things because we are who we are and being just that keeps our perception of what it is.

I've had the excellent opportunity to travel the world, most of the time for ministry. I've been to Romania, Haiti, Fiji, Germany, and India. But the people who have had the most impact on my life are the Filipinos. I've been to the Philippines seven times in the last twelve years, and each time I go, my worldview expands a little more. The first couple of times, I was trying to communicate and survive the trip. Once I embraced their culture, which didn't cause me to lose my way, I saw the world differently. I learned that it's not just spending time with people of a different culture; it's intentional about learning and embracing other cultures that broaden your understanding, which expands your worldview. Because of this, I treat people differently. I still have my values and moral compass, but the way I interact with people who don't look like me or do things differently from the way I am used to doing them has been transformed for the better.

A mile in another person's shoes can broaden our understanding of the world and how things work from their perspective. This would not only let us see things from their perspective; it would expand our knowledge of the world. **Often people who open and patronize charitable organizations understand what it is like to be in the other person's shoes and would do anything in their power to lighten the burden.**

Perception of Informed Behaviors

Some life experiences are personal to us, and this how we see and take in the world. It changes and forms how we see things in the world. With no prior experience regarding what others go through, we feel like we have a global view of how things work, but this all changes when we experience something new.

A friend told me about a time when she took her daughter, Laura, for an extended vacation out of San-Francisco, where they lived, and she said she thought the entire world lived there. She felt that she knew everyone in the world, but this changed with a fresh experience. As a child, she could make the changes because it showed her something new.

However, as adults, we pass every bit of information through the filter of experience. For most people, anything that does not conform to our expertise is discarded or given little value. When you are aware of who you are and when you will cultivate an awareness that there is more to life than meets the eye, you would be able to shape your worldview, which informs helps develop your identity.

A Pathway to a Better World

The world can only be a better place when the rigidity with which we hold perceptions is given room for diversity. This is not a call to lose your identity, not at all! Because we have to hold firm to certain things that make us who we are. But it is a call to understand better that variety is what the world is all about.

If you cannot try at some point in your life to see things from another person's perspective, then you would have lived life on an uninformed path when you had the liberty to move through twists and turns (without losing your identity or compromising your values) – all of which make life as sweet and exciting as it was designed to be. You may not believe in a creator, but I think that we were created for an adventurous life that includes discovery, setbacks, overcoming obstacles, change, and, most of all, lifelong learning.

Testing Your Worldview – a Path to Understanding Your Identity

The topic of your identity and how your worldview affects it is something that demands a high level of practicability. Now that the concept of your worldview is a little clearer, you need to take a piece of paper and write down your view of the world.

Once you have written this down, you have taken the first step to test your actual perception of how you feel things should be. Now also put into writing some crucial moments that have affected your life – the important ones, please. Then think of how they influence you and how they impact your thought patterns. Finally, think of some of the perceptions you now believe you need to change and write those down as well. The road to discovery begins with an inventory of what you have and where you are now.

Improving Your Worldview

From most of the things you wrote, there are some things you would like to change to have a better relationship with people, and also to have a better understanding of your identity. Who you are (whom you believe you are) plays a significant role in interacting with other people. Here are some things you need to do:

✓ Try to shelve one perception that you so dearly hold firm to for just a day and try to live that day through someone else's eyes.

✓ Try to see things the way they do and see how it would influence everything about you. You may notice how some things you hold so dear are very wrong. At the very least, you will have a fresh perspective.

✓ Take some time from your busy schedule to watch movies, read, and listen to music from cultures different from yours. Doing this would broaden your perspective of how life is – this shakes up your assumptions of life.

✓ Take some time to honestly reflect on your behavior, your choices, and your interactions with others. This is another way of changing the way you perceive life.

✓ Look for a fresh approach or even someone different from you to work with and relate to; make sure you are in tune with the differences between you and them. This would help you understand the world from a different angle because you hear, see, and do things differently.

The world can be a better place if only we will shake things up a little. Sometimes we hold so firmly to an identity that instead of bringing us together, only keeps people different from each other separated by retreating to their respective corners. **Does your identity prevent you from seeing the world from someone else's perspective?**

The lines we've drawn that prevent us from understanding others have also prevented us from enjoying the world more unusually. We are not created to set boundaries;

instead, make connections. These chords strengthen our bonds and allow us to explore alternative possibilities that not only favor us but make the world a better place.

With what I call string worldviews, we have people attempting to get things done on their own, without connecting with others, which most of the time is difficult. But if we were to intentionally make an effort to see the world through the eyes of others, we would be able to come together and achieve things beyond our wildest dreams.

Your worldview makes up the very depth of your assumption of life and the choices you make. If you step outside of the comfort zone created by your identity, you may find that you will enjoy life experiences beyond your wildest imagination.

Start by understanding your worldview and figuring out what you are all about – this is very important. Next, try to clarify your worldview so that others would understand and then try to see things from their perspective, and believe me, it is more fulfilling than you would think. For much of my life, I had painted myself into a corner by holding onto a perception that kept me from being fulfilled and achieving my purpose in life. However, with just a little purposeful effort to expand, it took me to a place I never imagined, and now my identity speaks for me; as someone with understanding rather than a one with a narrow personality.

144

CHAPTER 15

I SEE GOD

"Ask, and you will be given what you ask for. Seek, and you will find. Knock, and the door will be opened. For everyone who asks, receives. Anyone who seeks, finds. If only you will knock, the door will open." **- Jesus**

When I was very young, we lived in a poor neighborhood. I had to run home from school every day to avoid getting into a fight; we lived on welfare, and there were six of us living in a three-bedroom apartment. This was before video games, so we often played outside. One game we played was called *Rock Fight*. It's exactly what it sounds like, sort of like dodgeball but with rocks. You get the picture. The neighborhood kids and I were creative but left to our own devices; I'm sure that we would've eventually killed ourselves. Therefore, my mom felt the need to send me to Catholic school to ensure I had the proper discipline and a decent education. Twice a week, we were required to attend mass. Catholic mass was somehow simultaneously boring and intriguing to me. We kneeled, stood, chanted, sang, repeated after the priest, and genuflected, all in less than an hour.

However, on Sunday mornings, we attended a family church called The Holy Spirit Center. It was a stereotypical Pentecostal Black church. And unlike mass, Sunday morning service was "off the hook." There was loud singing, speaking in tongues, testimonies, and prayer, and that was only the first hour. Because we had not only exhausted ourselves but worked up an insatiable appetite after the service, we ate together. It was indeed a family atmosphere. However, when I considered the contrast of those experiences, attending Catholic Mass and Sunday morning services at The Holy Spirit Center left me wondering who God was? Was He this radical wild and crazy spirit, or the solemn old man type?

Ultimately, I had to find my answers to the questions many of us ask— purpose, creation, evolution, spirituality, and God. Because of the family environment I grew up in, I always assumed there was a God; I just didn't know who He was or what He was like. But I was eventually confronted with my uncertainty; is there is a God? And if so, is my perception of Him consistent with His reality?

By the time I began asking these questions, I had heard arguments for and against God. Those who didn't believe in God would state, "Since there is so much evil in the world, how can there be a loving, all-knowing God?"

I thought that was a good question, one I couldn't answer. But I also realized that there are two sides to every coin. So, another question came to mind, "If there is so much good in the world, how can there not be a God?"

I have not interviewed everyone in the world, but in my experience, people are not inherently good. In my experience, people do good and will sacrifice; but given a chance, at some point, they will always choose self-preservation over offering for someone else. Therefore, neither logical argument would satisfy my curiosity.

Someone once expressed an illustration that set me on a particular course leading to where I am today. He said, "Imagine that you lived in a time where there were no timepieces, no watches or clocks, and we used some other method, like a sundial, to tell time. You were walking and noticed a shiny object on the ground. You picked it up and observed that on the face were hands, and they were moving. You were curious, so you kept it and observed it for a few days. You noticed that every day it moved in the same sequence and eventually discovered that it tells time. When you shared your discovery, people eventually wondered where this timepiece came from. Is it more likely that you would believe that there was a certain set of circumstances where the element came together and formed this gadget that kept time perfectly? Or would you suspect that someone created this, and left it on the ground?"

For me, it was an obvious answer. There is no way that I would believe that this timepiece magically appeared after a storm or some other set of circumstances. It is too intricate; it has a purpose; it would have to have been made by someone. He said, "Now think of your hand, it has 27 bones: 8 in the wrist, 5 in the palm, and the remaining 14 are digital bones; fingers and a thumb. Think of how intricate it is; all the things you use it for and all different ways. Is it more likely that this evolved from an explosion somewhere in the universe, or that someone created it, with a purpose?" Like the watch, I concluded that it is more likely that is was created.

That illustration alone didn't convince me that there is a God. However, it set me on a path of discovery. Now, I do believe in God, and I think that Jesus did die on the cross for our sins for reconciliation. I don't think so because of scientific evidence; I believe, because of my faith in Him. But for me, scientific reasoning was the catalyst for my faith journey that led me here today—a Christian pastor who preaches Jesus.

My desire for you is to examine your perceptions of people and test how those perceptions affect how you treat them. And also, that you would embark on a spiritual journey of your own, to discover for yourself, that despite the evil in the world, that God sees you, just as you are, and He loves you.

I SEE YOU

ABOUT THE AUTHOR

Michael Carter is a two-time author and the senior pastor of The Life Church in Bloomington, Indiana. He is a graduate of Indiana Wesleyan University in Business Science and Religious Studies.

Michael has spoken to audiences around the world, including in the Philippines, Romania, and Fiji. He and his wife Detra have five children—four girls and one boy.

For more author information, visit www.mcarterlife.com

For speaking engagements, email mike@mcarterlife.com

Social Media: Instagram @pastormike129

MICHAEL CARTER

References

1. Emamzadeh, Arash. The Psychology of "Us-vs-Them." 2019 https://www.psychologytoday.com/us/blog/finding-new-home/201908/the-psychology-us-vs-them

2. Mendillo, Jenée. The 10 Benefits of Connecting Youth and Seniors. 2017 https://www.bayshorehomecare.com/10-benefits-connecting-youth-seniors/

3. Sapolsky Robert M. The teenage brain: Why some years are (a lot) crazier than others. 2018. https://bigthink.com/videos/what-age-is-brain-fully-developed

4. EnChroma & Valspar - Color for The Colorblind. 2019. https://www.youtube.com/watch?v=pWtv9pjiLWs

5. Merriam-Webster. 1828. https://www.merriam-webster.com/dictionary/race#h3

6. Merriam-Webster. 1828. https://www.merriam-webster.com/dictionary/racism

7. Kimberly Jade Norwood, "If You Is White, You's Alright. . . ." Stories About Colorism in America, 14 Wash. U. Global Stud. L. Rev. 585 (2015), https://openscholarship.wustl.edu/law_globalstudies/vol14/iss4/8

8. King Jr., Martin Luther. *Strength to Love.* Reprint. Originally published: Cleveland, Ohio: Collins + World, 1977

9. Monet, Claude. BrainyQuote. 2001-2019. https://www.brainyquote.com/quotes/claude_monet_176117

10. Varatos, John. BrainyQuote. 2001-2019. https://www.brainyquote.com/quotes/john_varvatos_612814

11. Merriam-Webster. 1828. https://www.merriam-webster.com/dictionary/judgement

12. Daskal, Lolly. 9 Valuable Principles That Will Make You Treat People Better. April 25, 2016. https://www.inc.com/lolly-daskal/9-important-ways-that-will-make-you-treat-people-better.html

13. Holy Bible. GOD'S WORD Translation (GW). 1995. https://www.biblegateway.com/passage/?search=Galatians+6%3A7-9&version=GW

14. Holy Bible. The Living Bible (TLB). 1971. https://www.biblegateway.com/passage/?search=Luke+6%3A37-38+&version=TLB

15. Thornton, Elizabeth R. "How Often Do You Judge People Unfairly? What Is the Cost?" The Objective Leader. 29 January 2015. Psychology Today. 26 August 2019. https://www.psychologytoday.com/us/blog/the-objective-leader/201501/how-often-do-you-judge-people-unfairly-what-is-the-cost

16. Khoddam, Rubin Ph.D. "Why Judging Others Is Bad for You." May 06, 2015. https://www.psychologytoday.com/us/blog/the-addiction-connection/201505/why-judging-others-is-bad-you

17. Merriam-Webster. 1828. https://www.merriam-webster.com/dictionary/friend

18. Marston, Daniel Ph.D. "Why You Don't Need Friends." May 08, 2019. https://www.psychologytoday.com/us/blog/comparatively-speaking/201905/why-you-dont-need-friends

19. Flora, Carlin. *Friendfluence: the surprising ways friends make us who we are.* New York, New York. Doubleday, 2013

20. Jauwena, Grace. "4 Ways to Tackle Loneliness." May 2019. https://lifeandhealth.org/mindfulness/4-ways-to-tacklelonliness/1515777.html?gclid=CjwKCAiAyeTxBRB vEiwAuM8dnYSk3CLXy7BfRD5LMzTGjLQWZtF7Q8qN uoGAABXG1O03dnLTrFq5XBoC3MgQAvD_BwE

21. Holy Bible. King James Version. 1604. https://www.biblegateway.com/passage/?search=proverbs+18%3A24&version=KJV

22. McIntosh, Peggy. "White Privilege: Unpacking the Invisible Knapsack" 1990. https://www.racialequitytools.org/resourcefiles/mcintosh.pdf

23. Ebbitt, Kathleen. "Why it's important to think about privilege - and why it's hard" 2015. https://www.globalcitizen.org/en/content/why-its-important-to-think-about-privilege-and-why/

24. "Holy Bible. The Living Bible (TLB). 1971. https://www.biblegateway.com/passage/?search=Acts+17%3A6&version=TLB

25. Delpit, Lisa. "The Silenced Dialogue: Power and Pedagogy in Educating Other People's Children" (Harvard Education Review, Vol. 58, Number 3, August 1988)

26. Astor, Maggie. "Young Voters Know What They Want. But They Don't See Anyone Offering It" The New York Times March 2020

27. https://www.nytimes.com/2020/03/22/us/politics/young-voters-biden-sanders.html

28. Bennett, S. (1997). Why Young Americans Hate Politics, and What We Should Do About It. *PS: Political Science & Politics, 30*(1), 47-53. doi:10.2307/420669

29. EEOC. (2019) Religion-Based Charges (Charges filed with EEOC) FY 1997 - FY 2019 https://www.eeoc.gov/enforcement/religion-based-charges-charges-filed-eeoc-fy-1997-fy-2019

30. Merriam-Webster. 1828. https://www.merriam-webster.com/dictionary/Christianity

31. Anor, Christian L. (2008) The Necessity for Change http://www.thetidenewsonline.com/2018/02/14/the-necessity-for-change/

32. Shahram Heshmat Ph.D. (2014). Basics of Identity. What do we mean by identity, and why does it matter? https://www.psychologytoday.com/us/blog/science-choice/201412/basicsidentity#:~:text=Identity%20may%20be%20acquired%20indirectly,to%20define%20themselves%20as%20worthless.

33. Overman, Christian. 2011. String Theory and The Voice of God https://biblicalworldviewmatters.blogspot.com/2011/04/string-theory-and-voice-of-god.html.

MICHAEL CARTER

www.ingramcontent.com/pod-product-compliance
Lightning Source LLC
Chambersburg PA
CBHW050724030426
42336CB00012B/1406